D1423342

PASTORAL VISITATION

DAVID SHORT WITH DAVID SEARLE

About the Authors

A Consultant Cardiologist at Aberdeen Royal Infirmary for some 25 years, David Short was appointed Physician to Her Majesty the Queen in 1977 and then Emeritus Professor of Clinical Medicine at the University of Aberdeen. In addition to his medical career he was both a preacher of God's Word and a pastor, particularly to the sick, bereaved and discouraged. His distilled wisdom and understanding were ministered to people of all backgrounds and nations and were conveyed with gentle grace and compassionate persistence. Together with his wife Joan, he prayed faithfully and systematically for the many whom God laid on their hearts. His chief desire was to see the Kingdom of God advanced by whatever means. He died in May 2005.

Until his retirement in 2005 David Searle was Warden of Rutherford House. Prior to that he pastored two Churches of Scotland before moving to Bangor, County Down in Northern Ireland where he pastored Hamilton Road Presbyterian Church for eight years from 1985. His other books include *And Then There Were Nine* (ISBN 1-58792-510-6) on the Ten Commandments.

PASTORAL VISITATION:

A POCKET RESOURCE

Designed for those visiting
at home or in hospital

DAVID SHORT WITH DAVID SEARLE

RUTHERFORD HOUSE
and
CHRISTIAN FOCUS

ISBN 1-84550-016-4

© Copyright David Short and David Searle

10 9 8 7 6 5 4 3 2 1

Published in 2004
Reprinted 2006
by
Christian Focus Publications, Ltd
Geanies House, Fearn, Tain, Ross-shire,
IV20 1TW, Great Britain,
www.christianfocus.com
and
Rutherford House,
17 Claremont Park, Edinburgh,
EH6 7PJ, Great Britain,
www.rutherfordhouse.org.uk

Cover Design by Danie Van Straaten
Printed and bound by Bercker, Germany

Contents

Introduction

THE VALUE OF A VISIT

Simply visiting and befriending a lonely person is a Christ-like act. The Master said: 'Whatever you did for one of the least of these brothers of mine, you did for me' (Matt. 25:40). It is impossible to imagine a greater privilege than that. Pastoral visitation and friendship are important, and essential for effective ministry. The basic requirements are to be there; to be sensitive to any particular needs; to be practical and helpful; and not to stay too long. The first visit is generally only the beginning of a pastoral relationship and there is evidence that additional visits are even more appreciated.

THE BEST GIFT TO TAKE

If a visit is to have maximum value, it must be a means of bringing God into the situation in some way. Have you ever noticed how Jonathan encouraged David? At a period of David's life when he was constantly on the move, a fugitive from the murderous designs of King Saul, we are told: 'Jonathan went to David at Horesh and helped him to find strength in God' (1 Sam. 23:16). Undoubtedly, Jonathan's friendship in itself would have been an encouragement. As a friend, he could have encouraged David by logic and argument, pointing to his skill in evading capture, or by promising to do all in his power to protect him from the king. But we are told he 'helped him to find strength in God'. How exactly he did this is not spelled out, but it could well have been by reminding him of God's promise implicit in his anointing as God's chosen king.

God's promises are utterly reliable, and the most valuable service we can render to those we visit is to help them to find strength in God, by leaving with them a relevant promise or statement from God's Word. The same applies to correspondence, whether by post or e-mail. The Word of God is a seed (Luke 8:11).

WHAT THIS BOOK PROVIDES
In the choice of promises and short Scripture passages, I have been selective. God's Word contains many great and precious promises – but not all the promises, when read in their proper context, are directly applicable to every circumstance in which Christians find themselves today. We are, however, able to use all those which remind us of the unchanging character of God, and also those

which are introduced by the word 'whosoever' or its equivalent. In the book, therefore, I have identified a number of suitable Scripture promises, which may be helpful in a fairly wide range of circumstances.

Those who are conducting pastoral visits must select one or two Scripture passages which are likely to be most appropriate to the special needs of the person to be visited. Because we may not fully know the circumstances of those we are visiting until we have actually talked with them, I felt it necessary to have a choice of Scripture verses. For instance we may go expecting the problem to be fear of an impending operation, and find the real problem is actually a sense of guilt. Since we do not know what we may find until we have spent some time listening during the visit, the best resource is to be familiar with several of the chapters in this book and then to be sensitive to the Spirit of God who promises his guidance. We should not assume that the one we are visiting has firm assurance of faith in Christ as Saviour.

I have concentrated on verses rather than on longer passages from the Bible, because they are more easily remembered, and can often be more easily grasped. That is not to say that sometimes longer passages of Scripture may not be appropriate.

I have added a brief comment under each verse to try and help in applying it to the person in need. In this, I have drawn heavily on *The Living*

Bible translation, on Eugene Peterson's *The Message*, and also on Charles Haddon Spurgeon's *Daily Readings*.

USE OF HYMNS

I have attached a suitable hymn to each chapter and suggested some other relevant hymn verses from the index at the end of the book. I believe hymns which make objective statements about God and his grace towards us can be valuable in helping us to memorise truth. It is significant to note that when God wanted to impress his warnings on his people Israel, he instructed Moses to write his message in the form of a song (Deut. 31:19). And what clearer justification of the use of songs of praise for encouragement than the Book of Psalms!

A problem may arise from the old-fashioned language of some of our great hymns. Many have been successfully updated, as in contemporary hymn books such as *Hymns for Today's Church* and the more recent *Praise!*[1]

However, some hymns lose their original character and meaning if they are significantly changed. We must remember that they have been a source of blessing to countless Christians over the years, and still have an immense power to encourage, comfort and instruct.

PREPARATION FOR A VISIT

All of us will often feel totally inadequate in trying to help those in need. In such circumstances, we must draw encouragement from the apostle Paul's statement 'I can do everything through him who gives me strength' (Phil. 4:13).

In attempting to focus on things spiritual, it can be helpful to ask those being visited: 'Do you pray?' If the answer is affirmative, then ask, 'What do you pray for? What special providences of God – in the sense of particular reminders of his care and concern – stand out in your memory?' Encourage them to count their blessings, and to name them one by one! Sometimes we can ask them what they would like us to pray for. The basic truths that undergird our pastoral ministry are that God knows everything that happens to us; his grace is sufficient for every need; he brings positive benefits from adverse circumstances.

Andrew Bonar's *The Visitor's Book of Texts* [2](sadly no longer in print) contains wise advice born of long experience. The following points broadly follow Bonar's instructions to visitors, though some have been altered slightly:

• Pray for the Lord's presence and the Holy Spirit's help.
We might echo the prayers expressed in Frances Ridley Havergal's hymns: 'Take my lips, and let them be filled with messages from Thee' or 'Lord, speak to me that I may speak in living echoes of Thy tone.'

• Make time for meditation and preparation beforehand – though the Lord is well able to bring an appropriate Scripture to mind in the course of conversation.

• Seek to win the sufferer's confidence: be really sympathetic, that is, being *alongside* them and taking a genuine interest in their daily concerns and family.

It may be worth asking if there have been any particular Scriptures or hymns in their mind, but we should not assume that a person's faith is resting firmly in Christ alone; they may be trusting in their own paltry efforts (see ch.18).

• As well as expressing the 'alongside-ness' of sympathy, try also to empathize, that is to imagine what it must be like to be in their situation; empathy will express itself in responses from the visitor such as, 'I sense you are feeling very lonely...' or, 'You must have been thinking there was no one who really cared...'.

• Be honest and faithful with the person you are visiting.

• Don't argue, though you may need to disagree – graciously and gently – with some things they say in order to resolve real difficulties.

• Try always to pass on a text from God's Word, spoken in his name.

• When visiting those unfamiliar with the Bible, it is usually advisable to start with one of the more familiar verses.

- If possible use a verse that has been helpful in your own experience – Andrew Bonar advises that the text should flow from our heart's fullness.
- Confine yourself to the simplest view of Scripture.
- It is a good idea to leave a card with the text on it.
- Pray earnestly with the sufferer.
- Words and prayer should always be brief.

There is a time to be silent (Eccl. 3:7), following the example of Job's three friends (Job 2:13).

David Torrance's advice regarding the prayer life of the pastor is most appropriate to conclude this section.[3]

- Pray every day for the gift of love.
- Pray to be conformed to the likeness of Christ.
- Pray to be filled with the Holy Spirit.
- Pray to be a good listener.
- Pray for wisdom and practical insight.
- Pray for courage.
- Pray that God will graciously work his miracles of grace.

David Short, Aberdeen, 2003

Endnotes

1. *Hymns for Today's Church* (ed. Michael Baughan), Jubilee Hymns, Torquay, 1982; Praise!, Praise Trust, Darlington, 2000.
2. *The Visitor's Book of Texts*, Andrew Bonar, Third edition, Edinburgh, 1859.
3. *A Passion for Christ*, David Torrance, Handsel Press, Musselburgh, 1999.

Chapter One
Hospital Admission

However 'routine' a hospital admission may seem to an outsider, and however calm the patient may seem, there is inevitably an undercurrent of fear that something *might* go wrong. So it is good that he or she should enter hospital resting on God and his promises. Fear is a natural human reaction to situations in which danger or discomfort is anticipated. It can be countered, to some extent, by rational reassurance; for example, by saying to the patient going into hospital: 'You are in good hands; your surgeon has an excellent reputation.' Similar arguments can be advanced in the case of other alarming prospects. But there is nothing to compare with the assurance of God's presence and support, and our total security in his omnipotent hands.

THE WORD OF GOD SAYS:
Fear not, for I have redeemed you... you are mine. When you pass through the waters, I will be with you; and when you pass

through the rivers, they will not sweep over
you (Isa. 43:1, 2).

We are precious to God. He paid an incalculable
price for our salvation. We belong to him. Since he
paid so much for us, he is never going to part with us.
Whatever happens, he will be with us.

Thou wilt keep him [or her] in perfect
peace, whose mind is stayed on Thee
(Isa. 26:3, KJV).

The great thing is to focus our mind on God, not
on our problems. It was when Peter, walking on the
water, took his eyes off Jesus and looked at the waves
that he began to sink – then Jesus caught him.

The LORD will keep you from all harm – he
will watch over your life (Ps. 121:7).

This is true for all who are pilgrims, with their faces
set toward the heavenly city.

Let the beloved of the LORD rest secure in
him, for he shields him [or her] all day long,
and the one the LORD loves rests between
his shoulders (Deut. 33:12).

Every child of God, however weak and failing, is the
object of God's unchanging love. We can rest secure
in his protection. There is no safety like that which
comes from dwelling near to God. Nothing can

harm us if we are shielded by him. We can just relax completely in him, like a cat on a warm hearth rug.

> We know that in all things God works for the good of those who love him (Rom. 8:28).

We can be absolutely sure that if we love God, however feebly, whatever we may go through will work for our good. We can say to ourselves: 'I am here by God's appointment.'

SUGGESTIONS FOR PRAYER:

- Pray for wisdom and skill for the medical team.
- Pray that the patient may be made a blessing to others and in turn be blessed.
- Commit those dependent on the patient to God's fatherly care.
- Commit the individual to the strong, loving arms of the eternal, all-sufficient and all-powerful God.
- Pray for a sense of God's peace and the realization that his children are infinitely precious to him. Where others, such as a medical team, are involved, pray for God's over-ruling.

PRAYER:

Father, we thank you that we are in your hands, whatever our circumstances. We thank you too for all the skill of modern medical science and the care and patience of those working here in this

*hospital. Give wisdom and skill to the doctors
and guide them in their work. Help us to know
a real sense of your presence and to be assured
that you never leave us nor forsake us. Be with
our loved ones and watch over them while we
are parted from them. So may our hearts and
minds be kept in your peace as we trust in you.
We ask all in the name of our Lord Jesus Christ.
Amen.*

SUGGESTED HYMN:

> Loved with everlasting love, led by grace
>   that love to know;
> Spirit, breathing from above, Thou hast
>   taught me it is so.
> O this full and perfect peace! O this trans-
>   port all divine!
> In a love which cannot cease I am His and
>   He is mine.
>
> His for ever, only His; who the Lord and
>   me shall part?
> Ah, with what a rest of bliss Christ can fill
>   the loving heart!
> Heaven and earth may fade and flee, first-
>   born light in gloom decline;
> But, while God and I shall be, I am His,
>   and He is mine.

ALSO SUITABLE: **57, 61**

CHAPTER TWO
Recovery from Illness

It is important that the glory should go to God and not primarily to the medical staff or to the patient's own constitution. The recovery should be seen as a call for a thankful response and a renewed commitment to service for the Lord.

THE WORD OF GOD SAYS:

Praise the LORD, O my soul, and forget not all his benefits – who forgives all your sins and heals all your diseases (Ps. 103:2, 3).

God's love and goodness have surrounded us from our earliest days, and every day brings fresh blessings. Let us not forget to praise him for them.

What can I give back to God for the blessings he has poured out on me? (Ps. 116:12, THE MESSAGE).

Thank God! He deserves your thanks. His love never quits (Ps. 136:1, THE MESSAGE).

> I am unworthy of all the kindness and
> faithfulness you have shown your servant
> (Gen. 32:10).

All God's kindnesses are sheer grace – totally un-
deserved.

> As [Jesus] was going into a village, ten men
> who had leprosy met him. They stood at
> a distance and called out in a loud voice,
> 'Jesus, Master, have pity on us!' When he
> saw them, he said, 'Go, show yourselves to
> the priests.'
> And as they went, they were cleansed.
> One of them, when he saw he was healed,
> came back, praising God in a loud voice.
> He threw himself at Jesus' feet and thanked
> him – and he was a Samaritan. Jesus asked,
> 'Were not all ten cleansed? Where are the
> other nine? Was no-one found to return and
> give praise to God except this foreigner?'
> (Luke 17:12-18).

> Thus far has the LORD helped us [Ebenezer]
> (1 Sam. 7:12).

We need constantly to recall particular evidences
of God's care and concern in our lives: 'Count your
blessings; name them one by one.'

He knows the way that I take; when he has tested me, I shall come forth as gold (Job 23:10).

It is wonderful to realize that God knows precisely the situation in which we find ourselves. But it is even more wonderful to realize that he has a glorious purpose for us as a result of the trial.

Suggestions for prayer:

- Give thanks to God and exalt his name.
- Pray for a fresh commitment of renewed health to his service, and an acknowledgement of God to friends and acquaintances.

Prayer:

Gracious Lord, we do want to thank you for your goodness to us in more ways that we ever realize or understand and especially for the real measure of recovery that has been experienced after this time of illness. We thank you for all the care and treatment received and for its effectiveness. But we thank you most for the consciousness of your guiding hand and life-giving power. As we face the weeks ahead, may the assurance of your presence and ongoing purposes for our lives be very clear, that we may continue to serve you all our days. We offer this prayer in the name of your Son, our Saviour. Amen.

SUGGESTED HYMN:

When all Your mercies, O my God, my
thankful soul surveys,
Uplifted by the view, I'm lost in wonder,
love, and praise.

ALSO SUITABLE: **18, 23**

CHAPTER THREE
Relapse or Continuing Illness

Prolonged illness, slow recovery and especially relapse lead inevitably to depression and discouragement. We should reassure the sufferer that God knows and cares, and that he has, in his own inscrutable wisdom, allowed it for good. We are encouraged to take all our needs to the Lord and seek his relief. If the illness is serious and if, following the directions given in James 5:14, the ill person requests a visit from the elders of the church, we should arrange that.

THE WORD OF GOD SAYS:

These [trials] have come so that your faith... may be proved genuine and may result in praise, glory and honour when Jesus Christ is revealed (1 Peter 1:7).

Faith untried may be true faith, but it is sure to be little faith. It is likely to remain immature as long as it is without trials. Faith is precious and its trial is precious too. We need not fear the testing because

the Lord has said: 'When you pass through the fire,
I will be with you.'

> Blessed is the man who perseveres un-
> der trial, because when he has stood the
> test, he will receive the crown of life that
> God has promised to those who love him
> (James 1:12).

The difficulty you are going through is a trial which
God has allowed to come into your life for a good
purpose. It will not last for ever. See it through with
his help and you will receive the hallmark of divine
approval, the victor's crown.

> Let us run with perseverance the race
> marked out for us (Heb. 12:1).

It is a tremendous reassurance to know that however
difficult or unpleasant our circumstances, we can say:
'I am here by God's appointment. My times are in
your hand.'

> The LORD upholds all those who fall and lifts
> up all who are bowed down (Ps. 145:14).

If we are bowed down by care, anxiety or ill-health,
he is able to lift us up by his almighty power. Can you
trust him for your soul and not for your body?

> We rejoice in our sufferings, knowing that
> suffering produces endurance, and endurance

produces character, and character produces hope (Rom. 5:3, 4, rsv).

Our troubles may seem pointless to us, but under God's hand they can develop our character, so that we better reflect our Saviour. We need patience, and here we see the way of getting it. You cannot learn to swim on dry land, nor can you learn patience without trouble. Tribulation, in and of itself, leads to petulance and unbelief. It is only by God's grace that it is made to work in us patience. Thus it is we are able to rejoice.

Unload all your worries on him, since he is looking after you (1 Peter 5:7, jb).

Worry, if carried to excess, is a failure to exercise faith and that must be wrong. If we cast our burdens on God, we will stay close to him. We must cast the whole of our burden on the Lord and not continue to carry a half, a quarter or even the smallest part.

Suggestions for prayer:

• Pray for help to commit our suffering, weakness, or depression to the Lord, and seek his relief
• Pray for the conviction that 'nothing is too hard for the Lord'.
• Pray for acceptance and patience if immediate relief is not his good and perfect will.
• Pray too for wisdom and skill for the medical team.

PRAYER:

Loving Father, thank you that in all our trials we are always able to come to you because your Son has opened the door into your holy presence. We ask that we may not lose the assurance of your wisdom and grace, but that we may be able always to trust you. We thank you again for the care of the medical staff and ask that you will be pleased to use the skills they have to work your perfect will. So may we wait patiently for you and be enabled each day and each night to rest in you, knowing that underneath are the everlasting arms. Amen.

SUGGESTED HYMN:

Be still, my soul: The Lord is on thy side;
Bear patiently the cross of grief or pain;
Leave to thy God to order and provide;
In every change He faithful will remain.
Be still, my soul: thy best, thy heavenly Friend
Through thorny ways leads to a joyful end.

Be still, my soul: thy God doth under-take
To guide the future as He has the past.
Thy hope, thy confidence, let nothing shake;
All now mysterious shall be bright at last.
Be still, my soul: the waves and winds still know
His voice who ruled them while He dwelt
below.

ALSO SUITABLE: 8, 11, 35, 45

CHAPTER FOUR
Those who are Facing Death

Andrew Bonar advises visitors to remind those nearing the end of their lives, of the past wonders of God's forgiveness, grace and guidance – the Lord has dealt so lovingly with us in all our many weaknesses and failures! So they can be encouraged to count their blessings, naming them one by one. They can also be reminded of their opportunity of helping by prayer those coming after, as Aaron and Hur held up Moses' arms until the army of Israel had won the victory.

For peace of mind, nothing is better than pointing the patient to the finished work of Christ. There is nothing we can do. All has been done perfectly and completely, and we can rest on that. Our hope rests upon the solemn promises of God, made to us by his prophets and apostles, and confirmed in the person and work of his dear Son. Inasmuch as Jesus Christ died and rose from the dead, we who are one with him by faith are sure that we shall rise again from the dead, and live with him. The fact of Christ's resurrection is the assurance of our resurrection.

Commonly, those who are dying have a feeling of total exhaustion. In his *Letters to an American Lady*, C. S. Lewis says: 'I think the best way to cope with the mental debility and total inertia is to submit to it entirely. Don't try to concentrate. Pretend you are a dormouse or even a turnip. Think of yourself just as a seed, patiently waiting in the earth; waiting to come up and flower in the Gardener's good time.' Harold St John said at the end of his life: 'I am too weak to pray, I am too tired to love Him much, but I'm just lying here, letting Him love me.'

THE WORD OF GOD SAYS:
This God is our God for ever and ever; he will be our guide even to the end (Ps. 48:14).

This promise of divine guidance involves life-long security, guidance right up to our last hour, and then endless blessedness.

When you pass through the waters, I will be with you; and when you pass through the rivers, they will not sweep over you (Isa. 43:2).

There is no bridge and no ferry-boat. We must go through the waters and feel the rush of the river. The presence of God in the flood is better than a ferry-boat. The sorrows of life may rise to an extraordinary height, but the Lord is equal to every occasion. We are precious to God. He paid an incalculable price for our salvation. We belong to him. Since he paid so much for us, he is never going to part with us.

> Even though I walk through the valley of the shadow of death, I will fear no evil, for you are with me (Ps. 23:4).

The presence of Jesus, the Good Shepherd, makes the believer independent of outward circumstances. A bright light may shine within us when it is all dark outside.

> My health fails; my spirits droop; yet God remains! He is the strength of my heart; he is mine forever (Ps. 73:26, THE MESSAGE).

> Peace I leave with you; my peace I give you (John 14:27).

Jesus bequeaths his peace to all his disciples. It is ours for the taking.

> Even to your old age and grey hairs I am he, I am he who will sustain you. I have made you and I will carry you (Isa. 46:4).

God made us and he will care for us. When we become a burden to our friends and a burden to ourselves, the Lord will not shake us off but will carry us to the end of our mortal life and into our eternal home.

> No eye has seen, no ear has heard, no mind
> has conceived what God has prepared for
> those who love him (1 Cor. 2:9).

Heaven is beyond our wildest dreams. 'We have a
brand new car waiting for us in the divine garage'
(C. S. Lewis).

> Therefore we do not lose heart. Though
> outwardly we are wasting away, yet inwardly
> we are being renewed day by day. For our
> light and momentary troubles are achieving
> for us an eternal glory that far outweighs
> them all (2 Cor. 4:16, 17).

'Outwardly wasting away' but 'inwardly renewed'.
Our present troubles, heavy though they are, are
'light' by comparison with the 'weight' of glory that
awaits us, and 'momentary' by comparison with the
eternity of heaven.

> Lord, now lettest Thou Thy servant depart
> in peace... for mine eyes have seen Thy
> salvation (Luke 2:29, RSV).

Once we have seen God's salvation, and are resting
on the finished work of Christ, we can sail into the
heavenly harbour in perfect peace. What can take
away the sting of death? Nothing but laying hold on
an unseen Saviour.

SUGGESTIONS FOR PRAYER:

• Thank God that though our heart and flesh may fail, he is the strength of our heart and our portion for ever. When we are too weak to pray, seek grace to relax in his love.

• Thank God for the finished, complete and perfect work of Christ in procuring our eternal salvation. He has done it all.

• Pray for faith to rest in Christ's work and not in our own totally inadequate achievements.

PRAYER:

'Though I walk through the valley of the shadow of death, I will fear no evil, for you are with me. Your rod and your staff comfort me.'

Thank you, Lord Jesus, that you have already trodden this road; thank you that you know the way and have promised to guide us in perfect safety to the Father's house. Help us to wait patiently for you in the assurance of the Saviour's victory. May your peace guard our hearts and minds and may our loved ones too rest in the certain knowledge that your grace is sufficient in every experience of life. We pray in the name of Christ Jesus, our Lord and Redeemer. Amen.

SUGGESTED HYMN:

All the way my Saviour leads me; what have I to ask beside?

Can I doubt His tender mercy, who through
    life has been my guide?
Heavenly peace, divinest comfort, here by
    faith in Him to dwell!
For I know whate'er befall me, Jesus doeth
    all things well.

All the way my Saviour leads me, cheers
    each winding path I tread,
Gives me grace for every trial, feeds me
    with the living bread.
Though my weary steps may falter, and
    my soul a-thirst may be,
Gushing from the rock before me, lo! a
    spring of joy I see.

All the way my Saviour leads me, O the
    fullness of His love!
Perfect rest to me is promised in my Fa-
    ther's house above.
When my spirit, clothed, immortal, wings
    its flight to realms of day,
This, my song through endless ages: Jesus
    led me all the way!

ALSO SUITABLE: 1, 35, 51, 61

CHAPTER FIVE
Bereavement

It is important to visit the bereaved person as soon as possible. This is the situation *par excellence* where love and support are far better than attempted explanation. The bereaved should be encouraged to be honest with God and not be afraid to tell him their feelings, even their anger. The truth is that the dark cloud always has a silver lining of divine mercy, if only we can see it.

One has to be prepared to answer the common questions: 'Why has God allowed this?', 'Will I see my loved one again?', and, in the case of the death of an unbelieving spouse, 'Do you think my loved one may be in heaven?' With regard to this last question, one can only quote the Psalmist and say 'The Lord is righteous in all his ways and loving towards all he has made.' There is the possibility that at some time (even at the very last moment) he or she may have called on the name of the Lord.

During a subsequent visit we can point out that the bereavement opens up a new phase of life and service. Initially, however, we are there to sympathize, console and listen.

THE WORD OF GOD SAYS:

As a father pities his children, so the LORD pities those who fear him; for he knows our frame, he remembers that we are dust (Ps. 103:13, 14, RSV).

God is like a father to us, tender and sympathetic to those who reverence him. For he knows that we are but dust, and that our days are few and brief.

Praise be to the God and Father of our Lord Jesus Christ, the Father of compassion and the God of all comfort, who comforts us in all our troubles, so that we can comfort those in any trouble with the comfort we ourselves have received from God (2 Cor. 1:3, 4).

Our experience of God's comfort in our sorrow enables us to be a blessing to others in a way which would not have been possible otherwise.

In all their distress he too was distressed (Isa. 63:9).

If you look up into the face of God, you will see tears running down his cheeks.

> A father to the fatherless, a defender of widows,
> is God in his holy dwelling (Ps. 68:5).

The reality of God's protection and fatherly care for widows and orphans has been proved on countless occasions.

> Cast your cares on the LORD and he will
> sustain you (Ps. 55:22).

God doesn't promise to take away the burden but to give you supernatural strength. Cast it on the Lord and leave it with him.

When the deceased was a believer

> We know that if the earthly tent we live
> in is destroyed, we have a building from
> God, an eternal house in heaven.... We are
> confident, I say, and would prefer to be
> away from the body and at home with the
> Lord (2 Cor. 5:1, 8).

When believers die, they exchange a fragile, draughty tent that soon wears out for a palace that will last for ever. What a glorious prospect!

> Blessed are the dead who die in the Lord....
> they will rest from their labour, for their
> deeds will follow them (Rev. 14:13).

To die in the Lord is to enter into rest.

When it is feared that the departed may not have come to faith in Jesus as Lord and Saviour

> The LORD is righteous in all his ways and loving towards all he has made (Ps. 145:17).

All God's deeds are governed by his justice and wisdom and love.

The loss of a baby

> [Jesus said] See that you do not look down on one of these little ones. For I tell you that their angels in heaven always see the face of my Father in heaven (Matt. 18:10).

Note the special provision God makes for his little ones.

SUGGESTIONS FOR PRAYER:

• *In the case of a Christian:* Give thanks for suffering and weakness ended, a work completed, and the reward anticipated.

• *In the case of an unbeliever:* Give thanks for the positive good accomplished, and the happy memories.

• *For a baby:* Thank God for the precious memories entwined around the little life, and for the fact that God has a special care for little ones.

• *For all:* Pray for supernatural comfort and strength to face the busy and the lonely days ahead.

PRAYER:

*Lord Jesus Christ, you have conquered death,
and for those whose trust is in you its sting has
been removed forever. Thank you that it is no
longer to be dreaded or feared, but that it has
become a gateway into the Father's presence.
Thank you that death is not a full stop, but only
a comma.*

*We thank you for every special memory
of our loved one and for all the love that we
shared during those years we enjoyed together.
We thank you that now all his/her trials and
weaknesses of this earthly life are ended. May
we have grace to say, 'The Lord gave and the
Lord has taken away; blessed be the name of
the Lord.'*

*Thank you for the comfort and support of
family and friends. As we face the future, may
we also know the consolation of your presence
and the assurance that for all who love the
Saviour the promise is that one day we too will
stand in your presence and be reunited with
those who have gone before us in that same love
of Christ. So may your comfort strengthen and
keep us. We pray in the name of Jesus, who died
for us and rose again. Amen.*

SUGGESTED HYMN:

Fear not, I am with you, oh, be not dismayed;
I, I am your God and will still give you aid;

I'll strengthen you, help you, and cause
  you to stand,
Upheld by my righteous, omnipotent hand.

When through the deep waters I call you to go,
The rivers of grief shall not you overflow;
For I will be with you in trouble to bless;
And sanctify to you your deepest distress.

When through fiery trials your pathway
  shall lie,
My grace all-sufficient shall be your supply;
The flame shall not hurt you; my only design
Your dross to consume, and your gold to
  refine.

The soul that on Jesus has leaned for repose,
I will not, I will not, desert to its foes;
That soul, though all hell should endeavour
  to shake,
I'll never, no never, no never forsake!

ALSO SUITABLE: **50, 51, 61**

CHAPTER SIX
Anxiety about the Future

We can point out that anxiety is integral to human life. Some individuals, particularly those with a sensitive nature and vivid imagination are more affected by it than those with a phlegmatic disposition. Our natural inclination is to try to avoid what we fear. This is not always good for our spiritual development. If we can learn that God really is all-sufficient and that his love does drive out fear, then we have advanced in our Christian life and learned a lesson which will stand us in good stead when we are called upon to help others.

THE WORD OF GOD SAYS:
Peace I leave with you; my peace I give you (John 14:27).

Jesus bequeaths his peace to all his disciples. It is ours for the taking.

The eternal God is your refuge, and underneath are the everlasting arms (Deut. 33:27).

God is eternal and unchanging. He is our refuge in the storms of life, and he upholds his people in his infinitely strong and everlasting arms. Can't you hear him saying to you: 'Peace, child, peace. Relax. Underneath are my everlasting arms'?

> God is our refuge and strength, an ever-present help in trouble. Therefore we will not fear... (Ps. 46:1).

A help that is not present when we need it is of small value. God is always present, effectually present, sympathetically present.

> Never will I leave you; never will I forsake you (Heb. 13:5).

This promise speaks for itself; the emphasis of the double negative is in the Greek original. God says: 'I'll never let you down; never, never, never, whatever the circumstances, and whatever your mistakes.'

> It is I; don't be afraid (John 6:20).

The disciples were scared out of their wits when they saw in the dark what they thought was a ghost. But Jesus reassured them: 'It's me. It's all right. Don't be afraid.' They took him on board and in no time they reached land.

> Don't worry about anything, but in all your prayers ask God for what you need, always

asking him with a thankful heart. And God's peace, which is far beyond human understanding, will keep your hearts and minds safe, in union with Christ Jesus (Phil. 4:6, 7, GNT).

We need to turn worry into prayer and thanksgiving.

That night the king could not sleep; so he ordered the book of the chronicles, the record of his reign, to be brought in and read to him (Esth. 6:1).

Sleeplessness is a great affliction, but God can use it for good. In the book of Esther, in the Old Testament, we are told of a king who had trouble sleeping, and turned to a book. This reminded the king of something he had forgotten, and this turned the course of history. Sleeplessness is also an opportunity for meditating on God's Word, for counting one's blessings, and for intercession.

SUGGESTIONS FOR PRAYER:
• Thank God that he is utterly trustworthy and that he does not put his children through needless pain or distress.
• Pray for a sense of peace and total relaxation in God's all-secure and loving arms.
• Pray for relief from sleeplessness, and for God's help to use the wakeful time for thanksgiving and intercession for others.

Prayer:

Lord God, you are eternal and unchanging and your love is completely steadfast and faithful. We thank you that in the Lord Jesus Christ and all he endured for us you have taught us to trust you in every experience of life. Forgive us that too often our faith wavers, and help us to learn to put our confidence in you as Jesus did in the dark night of his sufferings for our sake. May we too be able to pray, 'Your will, not mine, be done.' So may our hearts and minds be guarded and kept by his strong and loving peace. We pray in his Name. Amen.

Suggested hymn:

For the joys and for the sorrows,
the best and worst of times,
For this moment, for tomorrow,
for all that lies behind;
Fears that crowd around me,
for the failure of my plans,
For the dreams of all I hope to be,
the truth of what I am:
For this I have Jesus.

For the weakness of my body,
for the burdens of each day,
For the nights of doubt and worry,
when sleep has fled away:...
For this I have Jesus.

Also suitable: 17, 35, 46, 50

Chapter Seven
Fear of Losing Independence

If we live long enough, each of us will reach a stage when we can no longer care for ourselves. Then we shall lose much of our prized freedom. Our Lord predicted this in the case of Peter, saying to him: 'When you were younger, you dressed yourself and went where you wanted; but when you are old you will stretch out your hands, and someone else will dress you and lead you where you do not want to go' (John 21:18).

Being dependent on others, even when they are trying to help, demands our co-operation and involves loss of freedom. In such circumstances, we need to look to the Lord for his grace, and a spirit of acceptance and gratitude.

THE WORD OF GOD SAYS:
God will meet all your needs according to his glorious riches in Christ Jesus (Phil. 4:19).

God will take care of everything you need either through his servants, or supernaturally. His resources are infinite and his ways surprising.

My times are in your hands (Ps. 31:15).

Hour by hour, I place my days in your hand, and say with the hymn-writer: 'My times are in Thy hand, why should I doubt or fear?' and 'I am immortal till my work is done.'

> I lift my eyes to the hills – where does my help come from? My help comes from the LORD, the Maker of heaven and earth (Ps. 121:1, 2).

We need to lift up our eyes from our problems and our inadequacy and focus them on the unchanging, omnipotent God.

> Where can I go from your Spirit?... if I settle on the far side of the sea, even there your hand will guide me, your right hand will hold me fast (Ps. 139:7, 9, 10).

Wherever I go I'll find you are already there, waiting for me.

> Let him who walks in the dark, who has no light, trust in the name of the LORD (Isa. 50:10).

'I said to the man who stood at the gate of the year: "Give me a light that I may tread safely into the unknown." And he replied: "Go out into the darkness and put your hand into the hand of God. That shall be to you better than light and safer than a known way."'[1]

> Even to your old age and grey hairs I am he,
> I am he who will sustain you. I have made
> you and I will carry you (Isa. 46:4).

God made us and he will care for us. When we be-come a burden to our friends and a burden to our-selves, the Lord will not shake us off but will carry us to the end of our mortal life and into our eternal home.

Suggestions for prayer:

• Thank God that the Lord Jesus is the Good Shepherd. When he decides to move his sheep, he goes ahead of them.

• Pray for a peaceful acceptance of this fact.

Prayer:

Loving heavenly Father, we thank you that all our days are written in your book and that you know the end from the beginning. We thank you too that the future is in your hands and that you have promised your fatherly care will follow us all the days of our lives. Help us to face in faith the prospect of change, knowing that you go with us and will stay with us until the day when we see you face to face. We pray in the name of your Son and our Lord and Saviour, Jesus Christ. Amen.

SUGGESTED HYMN:

I do not know what lies ahead,
The way I cannot see;
Yet one stands near to be my guide,
He'll show the way to me:

I know who holds the future,
And He'll guide me with his hand;
With God things don't just happen,
Everything by Him is planned.
So, as I face tomorrow,
With its problems large and small,
I'll trust the God of miracles,
Give to Him my all.

ALSO SUITABLE: 8, 17, 50, 53

Endnotes
1. Miss Minnie Louise Haskins (1875-1957)

CHAPTER EIGHT
Worry about Loved Ones or Finance

Many people are more concerned about the health and prosperity of their family and close friends than about themselves. This is accentuated in cases when they fear that the loved one is hiding their worst experiences and fears, or when they are far away.

All we can do then is to commit them to the Lord in the confidence that wherever they are and whatever their state, the Lord knows and cares. We need to ask for grace to cast all our cares on him and not continue to carry them ourselves.

Most people go through periods when they feel they will not have enough money to provide for their needs and meet their responsibilities to those dependent on them. Many have experience of unemployment or redundancy, bringing with it not only financial anxiety but also a sense of failure, uncertainty and low self-image. However, God uses such experiences to teach us to trust him and to show us the blessings of being a member of the family of God. As a result of our experience of God's interventions, we become equipped to encourage those in similar trouble.

THE WORD OF GOD SAYS:
The LORD is my shepherd, I shall not be in want (Ps. 23:1).

This verse means what it says. If we belong to Jesus, the Good Shepherd, he will meet all our needs in all circumstances to the very end.

> Don't worry about anything, but in all your prayers ask God for what you need, always asking him with a thankful heart. And God's peace, which is far beyond human understanding, will keep your hearts and minds safe, in union with Christ Jesus (Phil. 4:6-7, GNT).

No worry, but prayer mixed with thanksgiving.

> The LORD can give you much more than that (2 Chr. 25:9).

If you have made a mistake, bear the loss of it; but do not act contrary to the will of the Lord. Be willing to lose money for the sake of conscience or peace or for Christ's sake. As Samuel Rutherford has said: 'We take nothing to the grave with us but a good or evil conscience.'

> God is able to give you more than you need, so that you will always have all you need for

yourselves and more than enough for every
good cause (2 Cor. 9:8, GNT).

Our need may be enormous, but God's resources
are infinite. As a result, we shall not only always
have enough for our own needs, but enough to be
generous to others too. Our duty is to trust God and
draw freely on the Bank of Heaven.

Blessed is the man who fears the LORD....
He will have no fear of bad news; his
heart is steadfast, trusting in the LORD
(Ps. 112:1, 7).

Blessed are those who are devoted to the Lord. If
we dread the arrival of bad news, how are we any
different from non-Christians? They don't have our
God to go to. They have never proved his faithfulness
as we have done. If we doubt his promises what is the
value of the grace we have professed to receive? So
stand still and see the salvation of God.

[Jesus said] I tell you, do not worry about
your life.... Look at the birds of the air; they
do not sow or reap or store away in barns,
and yet your heavenly Father feeds them....
See how the lilies of the field grow. They
do not labour or spin. Yet I tell you that
not even Solomon in all his splendour was
dressed like one of these. If that is how God
clothes the grass of the field, which is here

today and tomorrow is thrown into the fire, will he not much more clothe you, O you of little faith? So do not worry.... But seek first his kingdom and his righteousness, and all these things will be given to you as well (Matt. 6:25-33).

What a promise this is! Food, clothing, home and everything else you need, God undertakes to supply while you seek him. You mind his business, and he will mind yours.

SUGGESTIONS FOR PRAYER:

• Thank God he knows all about our loved ones and their needs, and their situation at this very moment. All that he does is guided by his infinite love and power and wisdom. We place them in his hands.

• Give thanks for the assurance that our Father will never let us down. We may have been unwise, but 'He knows our frame, he remembers that we are dust.' In spite of all our failings, he promises never to fail or forsake us.

PRAYER:

Eternal God, thank you that even before we bring our prayers to you, already you know all our needs. Thank you too that even though nothing is hidden from you, nevertheless you encourage us to share with you all our concerns and lay them at your feet. Forgive us that at times our faith is weak. Strengthen our trust in your promises to provide for our needs. Teach us the contentment of resting in the certain knowledge that you do care for us with the fatherly compassion and wise love revealed to us in Jesus Christ our Lord, in whose name we pray. Amen.

SUGGESTED HYMN:

Father, I place into your hands
The things that I can't do.
Father, I place into your hands
The times that I've been through.
Father, I place into your hands
The way that I should go,
For I know I always can trust You.

Father, I place into your hands
My friends and family.
Father, I place into your hands
The things that trouble me.
Father, I place into your hands
The person I would be,
For I know I always can trust You.

ALSO SUITABLE: **8, 9, 45, 50**

CHAPTER NINE
Need for Guidance

One day when I was waiting for my connecting flight at London's Heathrow airport, with thousands of travellers milling around, the thought came to me that among all the millions of inhabitants of the world, God knows insignificant me. God not only knows everything about each of us, but he is willing to guide each of us along the path to everlasting life.

When we do not know what to do, which way to turn, which option to take, it is reassuring to know we have a Father who is aware of our dilemmas. Nor will he allow us to make a mistake if we sincerely desire to do his will, knowing it is for our good and for the working out of his purposes for us. We need to soak ourselves in God's Word, meditate on it, and never go against its clear meaning. Things may appear to go wrong, and the devil may tempt us to blame ourselves for something we did or didn't do, but as we 'trust and obey', God will surely guide us aright.

THE WORD OF GOD SAYS:

Trust in the LORD with all your heart and lean not on your own understanding; in all your ways acknowledge him, and he will make your paths straight (Prov. 3:5, 6).

God has given us minds, and we must use them. But we must recognize their limitations. We need to ask for his wisdom and over-ruling in all that we do.

If any of you lack wisdom, you should pray to God, who will give it to you; because God gives generously and graciously to all. But when you pray, you must believe and not doubt at all (James 1:5, 6, GNT).

This is a wonderful promise. When we don't know what to do, God assures us that if we simply ask him he will give us the wisdom we need. We only need to ask – and trust.

We do not know what to do, but our eyes are upon you (2 Chr. 20:12).

Man's extremity is God's opportunity. None that trust in him are ever put to shame. 'The very dimness of my sight makes me secure.'

He guides the humble in what is right and teaches them his way (Ps. 25:9).

If we want to walk in the right way – God's way – we must humbly seek his face by reading and meditating on his Word and asking for his guidance.

As for God, his way is perfect (Ps. 18:30).

What a God! His road stretches straight and smooth. It may not be the easiest way, but it is the best way in the long run.

Let him who walks in the dark, who has no light, trust in the name of the LORD (Isa. 50:10).

'I said to the man who stood at the gate of the year: "Give me a light that I may tread safely into the un-known." And he replied: "Go out into the darkness and put your hand into the hand of God. That shall be to you better than light and safer than a known way."' [1]

Now glory be to God! By his mighty power at work within us, he is able to accomplish infinitely more than we would ever dare to ask or hope (Eph. 3:20, NLT).

God's ability to supply the needs of his children is infinite – far more than you would ever imagine or guess or request in your wildest dreams. Nothing – absolutely nothing – is too hard for the Lord.

SUGGESTIONS FOR PRAYER:
• Thank God for the gift of life with all its potential.
• Thank him that he knows all about us and has a perfect plan for our lives.

- Pray for a willingness to seek his plan and follow it.
- Thank God that nothing that ever happens to us is beyond his power to transform. Every stumbling-block can become a stepping-stone.
- Pray for help to drop our anchor into the depths of this truth.

PRAYER:

Lord our God, you have given us the gift of life with all its potential for good and blessing; we thank you that you have a perfect plan for each one of your children and that your way is always best. We thank you too that nothing in our lives is unknown to you and that nothing is beyond your power to transform. Indeed, even those things we find stumbling-blocks can become stepping-stones into your gracious purposes. May we learn to trust you fully, because those who trust you wholly, find you wholly true. All we ask is for the sake of your Son, our Saviour, who learned obedience through what he suffered and is now Lord of all. Amen.

SUGGESTED HYMN:

Cast care aside, lean on your Guide,
His boundless mercy will provide;
Trust, and your trusting soul shall prove,
Christ is its life and Christ its love.

Faint not, nor fear, His arm is near;
He does not change and you are dear,
Only believe, and Christ shall be
your all in all eternally.

ALSO SUITABLE: **17, 19, 27, 28**

Endnotes
1. Miss Minnie Louise Haskins (1875-1957)

CHAPTER TEN
Why has God allowed this?

Those who are assailed by doubt must not be allowed to feel they have betrayed the faith or surrendered to unbelief. The struggle with doubt is a sign of faith not unbelief. It is faith in two minds. This is when it is necessary to focus on the unchangeable, rock-like character of our God and acknowledge that his ways are unfathomable. We need to exhibit his faithfulness and love in our relationships with others, however unreasonable they may appear.

Being let down is something we all have to get used to. Being let down by a friend, someone we have been close to, can easily lead to bitterness. The antidote is to remember how privileged we are as sons and daughters of God. We have a Friend who is utterly faithful. Loneliness is not God's will for our lives. He may allow us to experience it in order to fit us to minister to others who are just as lonely as ourselves. Those who are lonely, and have been let down, need from us acceptance, affirmation and love, and the assurance they have them from God.

THE WORD OF GOD SAYS:

Jesus Christ is the same yesterday and today and for ever (Heb. 13:8).

Jesus never fails – and he is not put off by our failure.

We have a great high priest... one who has been tempted in every way, just as we are – yet was without sin. Let us then approach the throne of grace with confidence, so that we may receive mercy and find grace to help us in our time of need (Heb. 4:14-16).

The realization that our dear Saviour knows, by experience, all the trials and tests that we go through is a tremendous encouragement to go to him in prayer, in the confidence that he understands and sympathizes and will help us in our time of need.

[Trials] have come so that your faith... may be proved genuine and may result in praise, glory and honour when Jesus Christ is revealed (1 Peter 1:7).

Faith untried may be true faith but it is sure to be little faith. It is likely to remain stunted as long as it is without trials. Faith is precious and its trial is precious too. We need not fear the testing because the Lord has said: 'When you pass through the fire, I will be with you.'

God is faithful; he will not let you be tempted beyond what you can bear (1 Cor. 10:13).

God will never let you down; he will never let you be pushed past your limit; he'll always be there to help you come through it.

Cast your burden on the LORD and he will sustain you (Ps. 55:22, RSV).

God doesn't promise to take away the burden but to give you sufficient strength to carry it.

As God's chosen people, holy and dearly loved.... Bear with each other and forgive whatever grievances you may have against one another. Forgive as the Lord forgave you (Col. 3:12, 13).

Since you have been chosen by God, who has given you this new kind of life, and because of his deep love and concern for you, you should practise tenderhearted mercy and kindness to others. Be gentle and ready to forgive; never hold grudges. Remember the Lord forgave you, so you must forgive others.

Blessed is the man who perseveres under trial, because when he has stood the test, he will receive the crown of life (James 1:12).

The difficulty you are going through is a trial which God has allowed to come into your life for a good purpose. It will not last for ever. See it through with his help and you will receive the hallmark of divine approval, the victor's crown.

> As the heavens are higher than the earth, so are my ways higher than your ways and my thoughts than your thoughts (Isa. 55:9).

Not until we reach heaven will we be able to understand all the events that God allows to come into our lives. Even the most basic familiarity with the Bible (e.g. the life of Joseph) teaches us that much of what God's people experience cannot immediately be understood or seen as good. But if we take on board the truth of this text, it helps us to accept by faith that all things do indeed work together for good to those who love God.

SUGGESTIONS FOR PRAYER:

• Thank God his way is perfect. But he is so great and wise that our puny minds cannot understand the reason for all his actions. We walk by faith not by sight.

• Pray that as a result of our experiences, we may be able to understand and help others who are going through similar problems.

• Thank God that we are infinitely precious to him. We are his sons and daughters, even though others do not realize it. He has a wonderful future in store for us, and all the circumstances we are passing through, however disturbing, are preparing us for ultimate glory.

PRAYER:

*Lord Jesus Christ, you have experienced the pain
and loneliness of life in this fallen world, with
all its disappointments and grief. Thank you
that we may come confidently to your throne
of grace, assured that your mercy and grace are
available to us in our times of need. When it is
hard to understand, help us to trust you; when
we feel the pain of rejection, in your unchanging
love draw near; when we are overtaken by doubts
and fears, may we then prove your abiding
presence. Prince of peace, give to us the peace
of God to guard our hearts and minds through
your risen power. Amen.*

SUGGESTED HYMN:

I've found a friend; O such a friend!
He loved me ere I knew Him;
He drew me with the cords of love,
And thus He bound me to him;
And round my heart still closely twine
Those ties which nought can sever,
For I am His, and He is mine,
For ever and for ever.

I've found a friend; O such a friend!
So kind, and true, and tender!
So wise a counsellor and guide,
So mighty a defender!
From Him who loves me now so well

What power my soul shall sever?
Shall life or death? Shall earth or hell?
No! I am His for ever.

ALSO SUITABLE: **11, 22, 24, 41**

CHAPTER ELEVEN
Persecution or Feeling Slighted

When we feel slighted, it is a blow to our self-esteem. We feel wounded and humiliated. Often the slight is unintentional. Sometimes what is perceived as a slight may be a reasonable decision by an organizer to give someone else a chance to do a job. Sometimes intentional slights are a mild form of persecution, which Jesus warned his followers to expect as the norm. It is a comfort to remember that Jesus experienced everything from slights to the most extreme persecution. It is an honour to share in his reproach if we are genuinely being marginalized on account of our relationship to him. In such situations we need to draw our self-esteem from the fact that we are children of God. As such we must be prepared to forgive our enemies unconditionally.

THE WORD OF GOD SAYS:
Even if you should suffer for what is right you are blessed (1 Peter 3:14).

If with heart and soul you're doing good, do you think you can be stopped? Even if you suffer for it you're still better off. Don't give the opposition a second thought.

> Blessed is the man who perseveres under trial, because when he has stood the test, he will receive the crown of life that God has promised to those who love him (James 1:12).

The difficulty you are going through is a trial which God has allowed to come into your life for a good purpose. It will not last for ever. See it through with his help and you will receive the hallmark of divine approval, the victor's crown.

> Count it pure joy, my brothers, whenever you face trials of many kinds, because you know that the testing of your faith develops perseverance (James 1:2, 3).

Our troubles may seem pointless to us, but under God's hand they develop our character, so that we better reflect our Saviour. Because of this, we ought to rejoice.

> If you are insulted because of the name of Christ, you are blessed, for the Spirit of glory and of God rests on you (1 Peter 4:14).

Be happy if you are cursed and insulted for being a Christian, for when that happens, the Spirit of God will come upon you with great glory.

> Do not fret because of evil men.... Be still
> before the LORD and wait patiently for him
> (Ps. 37:1a, 7a).

Never envy the wicked. Rest in the Lord; wait
patiently for him to act.

> Blessed are you when people insult
> you, persecute you and falsely say all
> kinds of evil against you because of me
> (Matt. 5:11, 12).

When you are reviled and persecuted and lied about
because you are His followers – wonderful! Be happy
about it! Be very glad, for a tremendous award awaits
you up in heaven.

> No-one is concerned for me. I have no
> refuge; no-one cares for my life. I cry to
> you, O LORD; I say, "You are my refuge...."
> (Ps. 142:4, 5).

No one gives me a passing thought. No one will help
me; no one cares a bit what happens to me. Then I
prayed to Jehovah. 'Lord', I pleaded, 'you are my
only place of refuge. Only you can keep me safe.'

SUGGESTIONS FOR PRAYER:
• Thank God that he understands us and loves us,
and that we are precious to him. If we are the victims
of persecution, thank God for the honour of sharing
the reproach of Christ.

• Pray for a willingness to forgive, remembering how much we have been forgiven.

PRAYER:

Lord Jesus Christ, for our sakes you endured much suffering and contradiction against yourself, even to the extent of hatred, rejection and death. Strengthen and comfort us when we are slighted for the sake of the gospel. Enable us freely to forgive those who reproach us simply because we belong to you; may our patience in such trials point to you and even be the means you can use to draw others to yourself. Forgive us when we bring trouble upon ourselves because we have been thoughtless or harsh. Help us to keep close to you so that we genuinely reflect your likeness. May we live in such a way that we never bring shame but only glory to your great name. Amen.

SUGGESTED HYMN:

I heard the voice of Jesus say:
'Come unto me and rest;
Lay down, thou weary one, lay down
Thy head upon My breast!'
I came to Jesus as I was,
weary, and worn, and sad;
I found in Him a resting-place,
and he has made me glad.

I heard the voice of Jesus say:
'Behold I freely give
The living water; thirsty one,
stoop down and drink and live!'
I came to Jesus, and I drank
of that life-giving stream;
My thirst was quenched, my soul revived,
and now I live in Him.

I heard the voice of Jesus say:
'I am this dark world's Light;
Look unto Me, thy morn shall rise,
and all thy day be bright!'
I looked to Jesus, and I found
in Him my star, my sun;
And in that light of life I'll walk
till travelling days are done.

ALSO SUITABLE: **29, 34, 38, 69**

CHAPTER TWELVE
Does God Still Care?

Sometimes the feeling that God is distant and uncaring is due to our physical or psychological condition, such as a debilitating illness, clinical depression or even just a bad bout of 'flu. In other cases, it is the result of unrepented sin or neglect of our spiritual nourishment. Sometimes, God hides himself simply to increase our longing for him. Samuel Rutherford, the great Scottish divine, likened God's withdrawals to the night and shadows which are a benefit to flowers. We need to be reminded that God is unchanging in his love and goodness and is close to us at all times.

THE WORD OF GOD SAYS:
The LORD is near to all who call on him (Ps. 145:18).

Our God is always near; nearer than breathing, closer than hands or feet.

Let the beloved of the LORD rest secure in him, for he shields him [or her] all day long,

> and the one the LORD loves rests between
> his shoulders (Deut. 33:12).

Every child of God, however weak and failing, is the object of God's unchanging love. We can rest secure in his protection. There is no safety like that which comes from dwelling near to God. Nothing can come at us if we are shielded by him.

> You do not realise now what I am doing,
> but later you will understand (John 13:7).

We should not expect to understand all God's ways. He says, through the prophet Isaiah: 'Just as the heavens are higher than the earth, so are my ways higher than yours and my thoughts than yours.' Job didn't understand why he had to go through such terrible suffering, but God had his own reason for allowing it.

> Search me, O God, and know my heart;
> test me and know my thoughts. Point
> out anything in me that offends you, and
> lead me along the path of everlasting life
> (Ps. 139:23, 24, NLT).

We should always open our hearts to God's scrutiny, knowing that 'He who conceals his sins does not prosper, but whoever confesses and renounces them finds mercy' (Prov. 28:13).

I have loved you with an everlasting love
(Jer. 31:3).

We love him because he first loved us. His love is an everlasting, unchanging love, which is unaffected by our failures. There is nothing we can do which will make him love us less!

There is nothing in all creation that will ever be able to separate us from the love of God which is ours through Christ Jesus our Lord (Rom. 8:39, GNT).

Nothing, absolutely nothing, can get between us and God's love, because of the way that Jesus our Master has embraced us.

Why are you downcast, O my soul? Why so disturbed within me? Put your hope in God, for I will yet praise him, my Saviour and my God (Ps. 43:5).

Notice how the Psalmist takes himself in hand, speaking to himself, telling himself not to be cast down but to fix his gaze on God. If life isn't going smoothly, don't despair. As C. S. Lewis said: 'Troubles cannot cease until God sees us re-made or sees that our re-making is hopeless.'

SUGGESTIONS FOR PRAYER:

• What a comfort it is to know that the great God who sustains the universe thinks about each of us individually. The Lord of life watches over me and cannot ever forget me. My name is engraved on the palms of his hands.

- Thank God that his love never changes.
- Pray that if the breakdown in relationship is of my making, and I need to repent of coldness of heart or neglect of his Word, I may be helped to do so without delay.

PRAYER:

Gracious and ever loving God, we thank you that in Jesus Christ we can turn to you and call you 'Father', for you have adopted us into your family and made us one of your own children. Thank you that there is no going back on that and that our names are forever engraved on the palm of your hands. Come once more to draw us close to yourself, renewing in us the grace of repentance. Help us to turn away from anything that grieves you. Thus will you assure us of your steadfast love and restore in us the joy of your salvation, through our Lord Jesus Christ. Amen.

SUGGESTED HYMN:

He walked where I walk, He stood where
    I stand,
He felt what I feel, He understands.
He knows my frailty, shared my humanity,
Tempted in every way, yet without sin.

ALSO SUITABLE: 26, 37, 40

Chapter Thirteen
Lack of Assurance or
Feelings of Guilt

Feelings of guilt and fear of judgment may be due to an awareness of a past sin which is perceived as being unforgivable, or a fear that one is not among God's elect.

The answer is to recognize that none of us is good enough for God, that we remain sinners to our dying day. We are totally dependent on God's grace and forgiveness, purchased for us on the cross, and that God delights in mercy and forgiveness, and offers it freely to all. We need to be assured of these truths, and to pray with King David: 'Restore to me the joy of your salvation.'

Andrew Bonar emphasized the need for the pastoral visitor to take time to ascertain the real state of the person's mind, and specifically warned against denying the truth of election in order to counter the fear that the person is not one of God's chosen ones.

THE WORD OF GOD SAYS:

Whoever hears my word and believes him
who sent me has eternal life and will not be
condemned (John 5:24).

Those who believe are given eternal life as a present
possession. Note the word 'has'. All who put their
faith in God have eternal life here and now because of
the salvation which Christ has purchased. It is a great
reassurance to know that the Judge we shall face at
the last Day is none other than Jesus himself – the
One who loved us so much that he died for us.

If we confess our sins... the blood of
Jesus, his Son, purifies us from all sin
(1 John 1:9, 7).

Children of God do not need to make a confession
of sin as culprits or criminals before God, the Judge;
for Christ has forever taken away all their sins. But as
children, and offending as children, they need to go
before their Father every day and acknowledge their
sins. Let us lay hold of God's constant readiness to
forgive whenever we turn and confess our sins.

Blessed is he whose transgressions are
forgiven, whose sins are covered (Ps. 32:1).

There is no comfort or peace or security to be
compared with the assurance that our sins – those we
look back on with regret and shame, and many more

of which we are totally unaware – are totally forgiven and will never be brought up against us. They are 'cast in the depths of the sea'.

> LORD, you have examined me and you know me. You know everything I do; from far away you understand all my thoughts (Ps. 139:1, 2, GNT).

God knows the worst about us and loves us just the same. But he doesn't want us to stay the same.

> I know whom I have believed, and am convinced that he is able to guard what I have entrusted to him for that day (2 Tim. 1:12).

It is not a matter of what we know but who we know. Our faith rests simply and solely on Jesus Christ the Son of God. He loved us personally and gave his life for us, and his love never changes.

SUGGESTIONS FOR PRAYER:

• Pray for an ability to grasp the truth of God's promises – that through believing in him, we have eternal life as a present possession, and that Christ's sheep are totally and everlastingly secure.

• Pray that we may be able to re-affirm our faith, even if it means saying: 'Lord, I believe; help my unbelief.'

PRAYER:

Eternal and holy God, we bow before you in reverence and awe because, though your glorious majesty is unapproachable, you have done the seemingly impossible by drawing close to us in Jesus Christ. We thank you that in him there is full and free pardon and that we have been ransomed, healed, restored, forgiven. We worship you that when we see you face to face it will be because we are clothed in the righteousness of our Saviour who will be our Advocate to plead our cause before you. May we then trust only in him, assured that his forgiveness covers all and that for his sake you will embrace and welcome us into your eternal presence. Amen.

SUGGESTED HYMN:

Before the throne of God above
I have a strong, a perfect plea:
A great High Priest whose name is Love,
Who ever lives and pleads for me.
My name is written on his hands,
My name is hidden in his heart;
I know that while in heaven he stands
No power can force me to depart.

When Satan tempts me to despair
And tells me of the guilt within,
Upward I look, and see him there
Who made an end to all my sin.

Because the sinless Saviour died,
My sinful soul is counted free;
For God, the just, is satisfied
To look on him and pardon me.

Behold him there! The risen Lamb,
My perfect, sinless Righteousness,
The great unchangeable I AM,
The King of glory and of grace!
One with my Lord I cannot die:
My soul is purchased by his blood,
My life is safe with Christ on high,
With Christ my Saviour and my God.

ALSO SUITABLE: 42, 48, 49, 55

CHAPTER FOURTEEN
Carers

Carers carry a double burden. They share the sufferings, frailty and problems of the ones they are caring for. In addition, they have to cope with their own needs. The Christian community can be an invaluable source of help and strength to those in a caring role. Carers need to be encouraged to see their ministrations as being for the Lord himself. They should be concerned not only for the patient's physical and mental wellbeing but also his or her spiritual state and be careful to do nothing to undermine the work of the pastor.

THE WORD OF GOD SAYS:

The King will reply, 'I tell you the truth, whatever you did for one of the least of these brothers of mine, you did for me' (Matt. 25:40).

Whatever you do, work at it with all your heart, as working for the Lord, not

> for men, since you know that you will receive an inheritance from the Lord as a reward. It is the Lord Christ you are serving (Col. 3:23, 24).

We need to work hard and cheerfully at all we do, remembering that it is the Lord Christ we are really working for.

> Work for the Lord always, work without limit, since you know that in the Lord your labour cannot be lost (1 Cor. 15:58, NEB).

Our labour will be rewarded by the One who knows its real cost.

> Those of steadfast mind you keep in peace – in peace because they trust in you. Trust in the LORD for ever, for in the LORD GOD you have an everlasting rock (Isa. 26:3, 4, NRSV).

The great thing is to focus our mind on God, not on our problems. It was when Peter, walking on the water, took his eyes off Jesus and looked at the waves that he began to sink – then Jesus caught him.

> Those who look to the LORD will win new strength, they will grow wings like eagles; they will run and not be weary, they will march on and never grow faint (Isa. 40:31, NEB).

Looking to the Lord means focusing our eyes on Jesus and his perfect understanding of our need, and his total ability to meet it.

SUGGESTION FOR PRAYER:
• Give thanks to God for the service rendered, and pray for renewed strength and wisdom and grace day by day.

PRAYER:
Lord Jesus Christ, we remember how exhausted you often were as you gave yourself to all who came to you in need. In the midst of a raging storm, you slept in the bottom of a rough fisherman's boat. Thank you that you understand how we can become drained and empty by the demands made on us as constantly we care for those who are completely dependent on us. Renew our strength that we may not flag in our service. Refresh our spirits that we may work with patience and with joy. And restore our love that our task may done as for you. May the smile of your presence bring light into this home. We ask this for your glory. Amen.

SUGGESTED HYMN:
Teach me, my God and King,
In all things Thee to see;
And what I do in anything,
To do it as for Thee.

A servant with this clause
Makes drudgery divine;
Who sweeps a room as for Thy laws
Makes that and the action fine.

ALSO SUITABLE: **15, 16**

CHAPTER FIFTEEN
Loss of Faith

Although true believers are assured of eternal life, in spite of backsliding – of which we are all guilty at some time, in greater or lesser measure – the Bible teaches clearly that we need to watch and pray and to abide in Christ. As the writer to the Hebrews puts it: 'We have come to share in Christ if we hold firmly to the end the confidence we had at first.' It is clear from Scripture that many who appear to be Christians are not, so we should not assure backsliders of their salvation but emphasize the loving welcome from the Father that awaits their return, and the danger of persisting in unbelief.

There are many reasons for loss of faith. Some blame a feeling of having been let down by Christians – or by God – in failing to get what they earnestly prayed for. Others have found themselves drawn into a lifestyle, such as adultery or homosexual practice, which God's Word condemns. Yet others have fallen in love with possessions (Mark 4:19).

We should do everything possible to maintain a loving and caring relationship with those who lose their faith. They will naturally tend to cut themselves off from believers. Sometimes they can be persuaded to join another company of Christians. Commitment to helping a backslider is likely to be a long haul, so we need patience to keep it up for years. We need to persist in prayer, along the lines: 'Lord, take not your Holy Spirit from him/her; restore to him/her the joy of your salvation.' And we need to get others to join us in prayer for their restoration.

THE WORD OF GOD SAYS:

For we must all appear before the judgment seat of Christ, that each one may receive what is due to him for the things done while in the body, whether good or bad (2 Cor. 5:10).

We must all stand before Christ to be judged and have our lives laid bare before him, but those whose faith rests in God and in his Son, Jesus Christ, are safe.

Jesus told them this parable, 'A man had a fig tree growing in his vineyard. He went looking for figs on it but found none. So he said to his gardener... "Cut it down! Why should it go on using up the soil?"

But the gardener answered, "Leave it alone, sir, just this one year.... Then if the tree bears figs next year, so much the better;

if not, then you will have to cut it down"'
(Luke 13:6-9, GNT).

This parable reminds us what a dangerous thing it is if those who have had many privileges remain unfruitful. It reminds us too of the infinite debt we owe to God's mercy and Christ's intercession.

Jerusalem, Jerusalem.... How many times I wanted to put my arms around all your people, just as a hen gathers her chicks under her wings, but you would not let me! (Matt. 23:37, GNT).

This verse reminds us of the persistence of Jesus' love towards those who do not respond.

All day long I have held out my hands to a disobedient and obstinate people (Rom. 10:21).

Notwithstanding our disobedience and obstinacy, God goes on holding out his hands in invitation, waiting patiently for a response.

Jonah ran away from the LORD and headed for Tarshish.... Then the LORD sent a great wind on the sea, and such a violent storm arose that the ship threatened to break up (Jonah 1:3a, 4).

God didn't give up on Jonah when he ran away. He put obstacles in his path which were designed to bring him back and give him a new start.

When the son was still a long way off, his father saw him. His heart pounding, he ran out, embraced him and kissed him. The son started his speech: 'Father I've sinned against God, I've sinned before you; I don't deserve to be called your son ever again.' But the father wasn't listening! (Luke 15:18, 20, THE MESSAGE).

We have come to share in Christ if we hold firmly to the end the confidence we had at first (Heb. 3:14).

We must continue faithful to the end, trusting God just as we did when we first became Christians, resting wholly on what Christ has done.

Whoever comes to me I will never drive away (John 6:37).

There is no instance of the Lord turning away anyone who comes to him. It is not possible that you or I should be the first to whom Jesus shall break his word.

SUGGESTION FOR PRAYER:

• Thank God that his love is unchanging, and that he is ready to forgive and welcome and restore us as soon as we turn back to him in true repentance and faith.

PRAYER:

*Lord Christ, great Shepherd of your flock, who
went out to search for and bring back into the
fold with great joy a wandering sheep, come to
us now as we bow in your presence, and speak to
our hearts to tell us again of your tireless search
for one you love. Break down the coldness of
heart and melt the hardness which has driven
N... away from yourself. Restore him/her and
bring him/her back into the embrace of your
loving arms. Enable him/her to seek after you
again and to discover that he/she is only seeking
because you are seeking him/her. So may he/she
find the grace of repentance and faith in you as
Saviour, Lord and God. Amen.*

SUGGESTED HYMN:

There's a wideness in God's mercy,
Like the wideness of the sea;
There's a kindness in His justice,
Which is more than liberty.

There is no place where earth's sorrows
Are more keenly felt than heaven:
There is no place where earth's failings
Have such kindly judgment given.

There is plentiful redemption
In the blood that has been shed;
There is joy for all the members
In the sorrows of the Head.

If our love were but more simple,
we should take Him at His word,
And our lives would be all sunshine
in the sweetness of our Lord.

ALSO SUITABLE: **26, 42, 63**

CHAPTER SIXTEEN
Satanic Oppression

Satan is the inveterate enemy of God's people. He goes around not only like a roaring lion, but also very subtly. Sometimes God's people are aware (or strongly suspect) that they are the object of Satan's attacks. In such cases we need to remind ourselves of our Advocate on high who pleads for us before the throne. We need also to remember that Satan is a defeated foe whose oppression cannot last forever. He is like an animal that has had a fatal wound. He is doomed to die soon, but in his death throes still has some power.

THE WORD OF GOD SAYS:

Simon, Simon, Satan has asked to sift you as wheat. But I have prayed for you, Simon, that your faith may not fail. And when you have turned back, strengthen your brothers (Luke 22:31, 32).

It was owing to Christ's intercession that Peter did not entirely fall away. But it is not only for Christian leaders that Jesus is concerned. The apostle Paul reminds his

91

readers that Christ Jesus is also interceding for us, as is the Holy Spirit (Rom. 8:27, 34). It is wonderful to realize that we have an advocate beside the throne who pleads for us unfailingly and effectively.

> The God of peace will soon crush Satan under your feet (Rom. 16:20).

> The reason the Son of God appeared was to destroy the devil's work.... You, dear children, are from God and have overcome... because the one who is in you is greater than the one who is in the world (1 John 3:8b; 4:4).

> Your enemy the devil prowls around like a roaring lion looking for someone to devour. Resist him, standing firm in the faith, because you know that your brothers throughout the world are undergoing the same sufferings (1 Peter 5:8, 9).

Though Peter is most probably referring here to the fierce persecution about to overtake the church, his warning is as relevant today as it was when he gave it. Believers must always be vigilant and on their guard against Satan's attacks.

> Take up the shield of faith with which you can extinguish all the flaming arrows of the evil one (Eph. 6:16).

God has provided all his children with the shield of faith with which to ward off those blazing arrows which unexpectedly come hurtling towards us with deadly accuracy. It is by steadfast confidence in our Lord and Captain that every flaming dart will be extinguished and rendered harmless.

SUGGESTIONS FOR PRAYER:

• Thank God that his strength is supreme, and that he will not allow Satan to have his way.

• Thank him too that Jesus prays for us, and that his Holy Spirit strengthens and defends us.

PRAYER:

Lord Jesus Christ, we bless you that you resisted all the temptations that came to you during those lonely days in the wilderness as well as during your ministry and final passion and death. We thank you that having overcome the devil finally in your glorious resurrection, you are now able to strengthen and guide us when we are faced by his enticements and oppressed by his evil suggestions. Thank you that there is always a way of escape and that you never let us be tested beyond our endurance. Therefore, protect and guard us from all evil powers and may we be conscious that we are kept secure in your strong and loving arms. Amen.

SUGGESTED HYMN:

> Safe in the shadow of the Lord
> Beneath His hand and power,
> I trust in Him, I trust in Him,
> My fortress and my tower.
>
> My hope is set on God alone
> Though Satan spreads his snare,
> I trust in Him, I trust in Him,
> To keep me in His care.
>
> Strong in the Everlasting Name,
> And in my Father's care,
> I trust in Him, I trust in Him,
> Who hears and answers prayer.
>
> Safe in the shadow of the Lord,
> Possessed by love divine,
> I trust in Him, I trust in Him,
> And meet his love with mine.

ALSO SUITABLE: 7, 36, 40, 54

CHAPTER SEVENTEEN
The Sceptic

We should seek to win the person's confidence, and be really sympathetic and patient. It is important to try to understand why he or she came to adopt a sceptical attitude.

THE WORD OF GOD SAYS:
What good is it for a man to gain the whole world, yet forfeit his soul? (Mark 8:36).

These words of the Master should be engraved on our minds. It is possible to gain much but end up with nothing. Of all the unprofitable and foolish bargains that anyone can make there is none worse than giving up our soul's salvation for the sake of this present transient world.

Jesus answered, 'I am the way and the truth and the life. No one comes to the Father except through me' (John 14:6).

Jesus claims to be the way, the *only* way to eternal life. If we consider this to be too intolerant and restrictive, we should remember that he emphasized it in his Sermon on the Mount. 'Small is the gate and narrow the road that leads to life, and only a few find it' (Matt. 7:14).

> [Jesus said to doubting Thomas] 'Because you have seen me, you have believed; blessed are those who have not seen and yet have believed' (John 20:29).

The disciple Thomas was a sceptic. His ten fellow disciples all told him they had seen Jesus alive after his crucifixion, but he wouldn't accept it – until Jesus appeared to him personally; then he was totally convinced. It is not given to us to see Jesus with our natural sight, but millions down the ages have been convinced by the truth of God's Word and the evidence of changed lives.

> God was pleased through the foolishness of what was preached to save those who believe (1 Cor. 1:21).

God's way of salvation through the shameful crucifixion of Jesus seems to make no sense until by faith we realize Jesus died to bring us forgiveness, peace with God and eternal life. Then we begin to understand that the 'foolishness of God' is far wiser than human wisdom.

Jesus answered them, 'My teaching is not mine but his who sent me. Anyone who resolves to do the will of God will know whether the teaching is from God or whether I am speaking on my own' (John 7:16, 17, NRSV).

SUGGESTIONS FOR PRAYER:

• Thank God for sending Jesus into the world to be the way, the truth and the life.

• Thank him for Jesus' promise that if we really want to do God's will he will make things clear to us.

• Pray for the illuminating power of God's Spirit in our hearts.

PRAYER:

Thank you, Lord God, that you gave your Son to share our humanity, to become our Brother, to show us the meaning of life in his teaching, the way of life in his living and the secret of life in his dying. Give us humility of mind as we read your Word and clarity of thought as we try to understand. Your promise is that those who seek shall find. Create in us the desire to know you, and as we seek for you, guide us into a living relationship with Your Son as Redeemer, Saviour and Friend. In his name we pray. Amen.

SUGGESTED HYMN:
> Just as I am without one plea
> But that thy blood was shed for me,
> And that Thou bidd'st me come to Thee,
> O Lamb of God, I come.
>
> Just as I am, though tossed about
> With many a conflict, many a doubt,
> Fighting and fears within, without,
> O Lamb of God, I come.
>
> Just as I am, Thou wilt receive,
> Wilt welcome, pardon, cleanse, relieve;
> Because Thy promise I believe,
> O Lamb of God, I come.

ALSO SUITABLE: **10, 64**

Chapter Eighteen
The Self-Righteous

Andrew Bonar advises that we should try to ascertain the form of self-righteousness. Are they trusting in their decency, integrity, amiability, or is it in baptism or church attendance? They may be resting partly on rock and partly on sand. Our aim must be to lead the person to see that 'all our righteous deeds are like filthy rags', and even our best thoughts, words and deeds are defective in God's sight. Only the righteousness that God has provided in his Son, Jesus Christ, and which is received by faith, will pass God's scrutiny. 'God made him who had no sin to be sin for us, so that in him we might become the righteousness of God.'

THE WORD OF GOD SAYS:

But when the king came in to see the guests, he noticed a man there who was not wearing wedding clothes. 'Friend,' he asked, 'how did you get in here without wedding clothes?' The man was speechless (Matt. 22:11, 12).

None of us can appear before the holy God in our own righteousness. It would be utterly unthinkable. God has provided a perfect righteousness through the life and death and resurrection of his Son, Jesus Christ. Rejecting that can only mean eternal loss.

> We are utterly incapable of living the glorious lives God wills for us (Rom. 3:23, THE MESSAGE).

Not only have we failed to attain God's standard in the past, we are totally unable to do so in the future in our own strength.

> I know that nothing good lives in me, that is, in my sinful nature (Rom. 7:18a).

We are like seemingly attractive apples which are in reality rotten at the core and unfit for consumption.

> But whatever was to my profit I now consider loss for the sake of Christ. What is more, I consider everything a loss compared to the surpassing greatness of knowing Christ Jesus my Lord, for whose sake I have lost all things. I consider them rubbish, that I may gain Christ and be found in him, not having a righteousness of my own that comes from the law, but that which is through faith in Christ — the rightousness that comes from God and is by faith (Phil. 3:7-9).

This is what the LORD says: 'Let not the
wise man boast of his wisdom or the strong
man boast of his strength or the rich man
boast of his riches, but let him who boasts
boast about this: that he understands and
knows me...' (Jer. 9:23, 24a).

Not our wisdom nor any other of our attainments can
make us acceptable to God. Our only security lies in
knowing God, believing him and being reconciled to
him through his Son, Jesus Christ.

PRAYER:

*Lord, help us to see ourselves as you see us:
good, because you have made us in the divine
image; but not good enough, because we are
totally unable to reach your standard without
your help. Have mercy on us, we pray, and lead
us to put our faith in Christ's righteousness and
his alone.*

SUGGESTED HYMN:

My hope is built on nothing less
Than Jesus' blood and righteousness;
I dare not trust the sweetest frame,
But wholly lean on Jesus' name.

*On Christ, the solid Rock, I stand;
All other ground is sinking sand.*

When darkness seems to veil his face,
I rest on his unchanging grace;
In every high and stormy gale,
My anchor holds within the veil.

ALSO SUITABLE: 7, 55

CHAPTER NINETEEN
Spiritual State Unknown

In situations where we do not know the precise spiritual state of the one we are visiting, we are supremely dependent on the guidance of the Holy Spirit. The question: 'Are you able to pray about your problem?' will usually indicate where they stand in relation to God. Andrew Bonar makes the point that the sufferer will often hope that the minister will pray for him/her – believing it might have a magical effect on his or her condition. What is needed even more than prayer is a clear and loving expression of God's truth.

THE WORD OF GOD SAYS:

The LORD is good, a refuge in times of trouble. He cares for those who trust in him (Nahum 1:7).

The Lord is good, uniquely good – 'No one is good, except God alone' – and he is an unfailing refuge for those in trouble.

We all, like sheep, have gone astray, each of us has turned to his own way; and the

> LORD has laid on him the iniquity of us all
> (Isa. 53:6).

We are all different, but we are all alike in that we go astray from God's ways, and refuse to obey him. But amazingly, instead of punishing us, as we deserve, he took the punishment himself, by coming into our world and dying on the cross.

> God so loved the world that he gave his one and only Son, that whoever believes in him shall not perish but have eternal life (John 3:16).

God loved men and women so much that he gave his only Son to suffer death on the cross and bear the punishment of our sins so that we might be forgiven and have eternal life – simply through faith in Christ.

> We must all appear before the judgment seat of Christ, that each one may receive what is due him for the things done while in the body, whether good or bad. Jesus said: 'I tell you the truth, whoever hears my word and believes him who sent me has eternal life and will not be condemned.' (2 Cor. 5:10; John 5:24).

We must all stand before Christ to be judged and have our lives laid bare before him, but, says Jesus,

'Anyone who listens to my message, and believes in God who sent me has eternal life and will never be condemned for his sins.'

SUGGESTIONS FOR PRAYER:

• Thank God that he is good; the only true refuge in time of trouble.

• Thank him for his amazing love for this world shown in the gift of his unique Son to suffer death on the cross for our salvation.

• Pray that we may respond to his love in true repentance and faith.

PRAYER:

Gracious and loving God, we cannot understand how or why you should love us so much when we have often turned away from you and gone our own way, deliberately flying in the face of your holy commandments. Yet in our sinfulness, you have come to us through your Son, the Lord Jesus Christ, and he has carried in himself on the cross the just penalty of our rebellion. Help us now to see him hanging there in our place, so that we might go free. Give us the gift of faith that we might trust him for his forgiveness. And bring to us the strong assurance of your pardon and the certain knowledge that for his sake you welcome us into your family as your children. We ask this in his name. Amen.

Suggested hymn:

Eternal Light! Eternal Light!
How pure the soul must be,
When placed within Thy searching sight,
It shrinks not, but, with calm delight,
Can live and look on Thee!

The spirits that surround Thy throne
May bear the burning bliss;
But that is surely theirs alone,
Since they have never, never known
A fallen world like this.

O how shall I, whose native sphere
Is dark, whose mind is dim,
Before the Ineffable appear,
And on my naked spirit bear
The uncreated beam?

There is a way for man to rise
To that sublime abode:
An offering and a sacrifice,
A Holy Spirit's energies,
An Advocate with God.

These, these prepare us for the sight
Of holiness above:
The sons of ignorance and night
May dwell in the eternal Light,
Through the eternal Love!

Also suitable: 7, 39, 42, 62

CHAPTER TWENTY
Anniversaries and Congratulations

Anniversaries remind us of the goodness of God, and of his blessings on us in the past. In some cases they may recall sorrows and losses – but always under the overarching faithfulness of God, who gives us far more than we deserve. Anniversaries also remind us of the passing of time and the approaching return of Christ and our summons to the judgment seat of Christ; perhaps also of reducing strength and diminishing opportunities of service for the Master.

It is our privilege and duty as Christians to rejoice with those who rejoice and to thank God for the success he has granted. Success often opens new doors of opportunity, and it is frequently appropriate to recall God's Word: 'Those who honour me I will honour, but those who despise me will be disdained.' An engagement or the birth of a child or grandchild will demand a commitment to long-term prayer.

THE WORD OF GOD SAYS:

I trust in your unfailing love; my heart rejoices in your salvation. I will sing to the LORD, for he has been good to me (Ps. 13:5, 6).

As we recall God's mercies and blessings in the past, we have solid grounds for trusting him in the present and for rejoicing as we look into the future.

You have made known to me the path of life; you will fill me with joy in your presence, with eternal pleasures at your right hand (Ps. 16:11).

If, by God's grace, our feet have been set on the path of life, the future is glorious.

The LORD sends poverty and wealth; he humbles and he exalts (1 Sam. 2:7).

All that I am, he made me. All that I have, he gave me.

Great is your faithfulness (Lam. 3:23b).

Jeremiah could say this even when he contemplated the loss of all that he loved most dearly. God is faithful and will remain faithful whatever the outward appearances.

My cup overflows. Surely goodness and love will follow me all the days of my life (Ps. 23:5b, 6).

God's blessings are not just a full cup but a cup running over – like an overflowing head on a refreshing drink! His blessings will never fail. His goodness will continue to supply our needs and his steadfast love and mercy will continue to blot out our sins.

> Every good and perfect gift is from above, coming down from the Father of the heavenly lights, who does not change like shifting shadows (James 1:17).

We should not only rejoice in our blessings, we should trace the sunbeams up to their source in the Sun of Righteousness, whose love is constant and unfailing.

SUGGESTIONS FOR PRAYER:

• Thank God for his unchanging faithfulness and love in spite of our many failures.

• Pray for a fresh resolve to serve him better in the days ahead.

• Thank God for his blessing, recognizing that however hard we may work, success comes ultimately from God and God alone.

• Pray for grace to build on the success granted, and to move forward in God's service.

PRAYER:

'How good is the God we adore, our faithful, unchangeable Friend!' We bless you, our Lord God, for your loving faithfulness down the years,

and for the occasion that brings us together
today. Thank you that your mercies have never
failed, but are new and fresh every morning.
Thank you that 'Through many dangers, toils
and snares, we have already come, 'tis grace that
brought us safe thus far, and grace will lead us
home.' Accept the thanksgiving and praise we
bring and may we always give you all the glory.
We pray in and through your Son, our Lord and
Saviour. Amen.

SUGGESTED HYMN:

Great is Thy faithfulness, O God my Father,
There is no shadow of turning with Thee;
Thou changest not, Thy compassions they
    fail not,
As Thou hast been Thou for ever wilt be.

*Great is Thy faithfulness, great is Thy faithful-
    ness;*
Morning by morning new mercies I see;
All I have needed Thy hand hath provided
Great is Thy faithfulness, Lord, unto me!

ALSO SUITABLE: 18, 23, 68

Alphabetical index
of hymn verses

1. Abide with me; fast falls the eventide:
    The darkness deepens; Lord, with me abide;
    When other helpers fail, and comforts flee,
    Help of the helpless, O abide with me.

    Swift to its close ebbs out life's little day;
    Earth's joys grow dim, its glories pass away;
    Change and decay in all around I see;
    O Thou who changest not, abide with me.
    Henry Francis Lyte (1793-1847)

2. All my hope on God is founded;
    He doth still my trust renew,
    Me through change and chance He guideth,
    Only good and only true.
    God unknown,
    He alone
    Calls my heart to be His own.
    Joachim Neander (1650-80)

3. All the way my Saviour leads me;
    What have I to ask beside?

Can I doubt His tender mercy,
Who through life has been my guide?
Heavenly peace, divinest comfort,
Here by faith in Him to dwell!
For I know whate'er befall me,
Jesus doeth all things well.

All the way my Saviour leads me,
Cheers each winding path I tread,
Gives me grace for every trial,
Feeds me with the living bread.
Though my weary steps may falter,
And my soul a-thirst may be,
Gushing from the rock before me,
Lo! a spring of joy I see.

All the way my Saviour leads me,
O the fullness of His love!
Perfect rest to me is promised
In my Father's house above.
When my spirit, clothed, immortal,
Wings its flight to realms of day,
This, my song through endless ages:
Jesus led me all the way!

Fanny Crosby (1820-1915)

4. Amazing grace! how sweet the sound
That saved a wretch like me:
I once was lost, but now am found;
Was blind but now I see.

John Newton (1725-1807)

5. And when the strife is fierce, the warfare long,
   Steals on the ear the distant triumph song,
   And hearts are brave again, and arms are strong.
   Hallelujah!

   William Walsham How (1823-97)

6. Be still, my soul: The Lord is on thy side;
   Bear patiently the cross of grief or pain;
   Leave to thy God to order and provide;
   In every change He faithful will remain.
   Be still, my soul: thy best, thy heavenly Friend
   Through thorny ways leads to a joyful end.

   Be still, my soul: thy God doth undertake
   To guide the future as He has the past.
   Thy hope, thy confidence, let nothing shake;
   All now mysterious shall be bright at last.
   Be still, my soul: the waves and winds still know
   His voice who ruled them while He dwelt below.

   Katharina von Schlegel (b.1697) tr. Jane Borthwick (1813-97)

7. Before the throne of God above
   I have a strong, a perfect plea:
   A great High Priest whose name is Love,
   Who ever lives and pleads for me.
   My name is written on his hands,
   My name is hidden in his heart;
   I know that while in heaven he stands
   No power can force me to depart.

When Satan tempts me to despair
And tells me of the guilt within,
Upward I look, and see him there
Who made an end to all my sin.
Because the sinless Saviour died,
My sinful soul is counted free;
For God, the just, is satisfied
To look on him and pardon me.

Behold him there! The risen Lamb,
My perfect, sinless Righteousness,
The great unchangeable I AM,
The King of glory and of grace!
One with my Lord I cannot die:
My soul is purchased by his blood,
My life is safe with Christ on high,
With Christ my Saviour and my God.

Charitie Lees Bancroft (1841-1923)

8. Cast care aside, lean on your Guide,
His boundless mercy will provide;
Trust, and your trusting soul shall prove,
Christ is its life and Christ its love.

Faint not, nor fear, His arm is near;
He does not change and you are dear,
Only believe, and Christ shall be
Your all in all eternally.

John Samuel Bewley Monsell (1811-75)

9. Christ is the answer to my every need;
Christ is the answer, He is my friend indeed.
Problems of life my spirit may assail,
With Christ my Saviour I need never fail,
For Christ is the answer to my need.

Anon

10. Eternal Light! Eternal Light!
How pure the soul must be,
When placed within Thy searching sight,
It shrinks not, but, with calm delight,
Can live and look on Thee!

The spirits that surround Thy throne
May bear the burning bliss;
But that is surely theirs alone,
Since they have never, never known
A fallen world like this.

O how shall I, whose native sphere
Is dark, whose mind is dim,
Before the Ineffable appear,
And on my naked spirit bear
The uncreated beam?

There is a way for man to rise
To that sublime abode:
An offering and a sacrifice,
A Holy Spirit's energies,
An Advocate with God.

These, these prepare us for the sight
Of holiness above:
The sons of ignorance and night
May dwell in the eternal Light,
Through the eternal Love!

Thomas Binney (1798-1874)

11. Faithful One, so unchanging;
Ageless One, You're my rock of peace.
Lord of all, I depend on You,
I call out to you again and again.

You are my rock in times of trouble,
You lift me up when I fall down;
All through the storm,
Your love is the anchor –
My hope is in You alone.

Brian Doerksen © 1989 Vineyard Publishing

12. Father, I place into your hands
The things that I can't do.
Father, I place into your hands
The times that I've been through.
Father, I place into your hands
The way that I should go,
For I know I always can trust You.

Father, I place into your hands
My friends and family.
Father, I place into your hands

The things that trouble me.
Father, I place into your hands
The person I would be,
For I know I always can trust You.

Jenny Hewer © Kingsway

13. Fear not, I am with you, oh, be not dismayed;
I, I am your God and will still give you aid;
I'll strengthen you, help you, and cause you to stand,
Upheld by my righteous, omnipotent hand.

When through the deep waters I call you to go,
The rivers of grief shall not you overflow;
For I will be with you in trouble to bless;
And sanctify to you your deepest distress.

When through fiery trials your pathway shall lie,
My grace all-sufficient shall be your supply;
The flame shall not hurt you; my only design
Your dross to consume, and your gold to refine.

The soul that on Jesus has leaned for repose,
I will not, I will not, desert to its foes;
That soul, though all hell should endeavour to shake,
I'll never, no never, no never forsake!

Richard Keen (c.1787)

14. For the joys and for the sorrows,
The best and worst of times,
For this moment, for tomorrow,
For all that lies behind;

Fears that crowd around me,
For the failure of my plans,
For the dreams of all I hope to be,
The truth of what I am:
For this I have Jesus.

For the weakness of my body,
The burdens of each day,
For the nights of doubt and worry,
When sleep has fled away:
Needing reassurance,
And the will to start again,
A steely-eyed endurance,
The Strength to fight and win:
For this I have Jesus.

Graham Kendrick © 1994 Make Way Music

15. Forth in Thy name, O Lord, I go,
My daily labour to pursue,
Thee, only Thee, resolved to know,
In all I think, or speak, or do.

The task Thy wisdom has assigned
O let me cheerfully fulfil;
In all my works Thy presence find,
And prove Thy good and perfect will.

Charles Wesley (1707-88)

16. Go, labour on; spend and be spent,
Thy joy to do the Father's will;
It is the way the Master went;
Should not the servant tread it still?

Horatius Bonar (1808-89)

17. God holds the key of all unknown,
   And I am glad:
   If other hands should hold the key,
   Or if He trusted it to me,
   I might be sad.

   The very dimness of my sight
   Makes me secure;
   For, groping in my misty way,
   I feel His hand; I hear Him say,
   'My help is sure'.

   Joseph Parker (1830-1902)

18. God is good – we sing and shout it,
   God is good – we celebrate;
   God is good – no more we doubt it,
   God is good – we know it's true!
   Graham Kendrick © 1985 Thankyou Music

19. God moves in a mysterious way,
   His wonders to perform;
   He plants His footsteps in the sea,
   And rides upon the storm.

   Deep in unfathomable mines
   Of never-failing skill,
   He treasures up his bright designs,
   And works His sovereign will.
   William Cowper (1731-1800)

20. Great is Thy faithfulness, O God my Father,
There is no shadow of turning with Thee;
Thou changest not, Thy compassions they fail not,
As Thou hast been Thou for ever wilt be.

Great is Thy faithfulness, great is Thy faithfulness;
Morning by morning new mercies I see;
All I have needed Thy hand hath provided
Great is Thy faithfulness, Lord, unto me!
                    Thomas O. Chisholm (1866-1960)

21. Have Thine own way, Lord, have Thine own way;
Thou art the potter, I am the clay;
Mould me and make me after Thy will,
While I am waiting, yielded and still.
                    A. A. Pollard (1862-1934)

22. He walked where I walk, He stood where I stand,
He felt what I feel, He understands.
He knows my frailty, shared my humanity,
Tempted in every way, yet without sin.
                    Graham Kendrick © 1988 Make Way Music

23. How good is the God we adore,
Our faithful, unchangeable Friend!
His love is as great as His power,
And knows neither measure nor end!

'Tis Jesus the First and the Last,
Whose Spirit shall guide us safe home;

We'll praise Him for all that is past,
We'll trust Him for all that's to come.
Joseph Hart (1712-68)

24. How sweet the name of Jesus sounds
    In a believer's ear!
    It soothes his sorrows, heals his wounds,
    And drives away his fear.

    It makes the wounded spirit whole,
    And calms the troubled breast;
    It satisfies the hungry soul,
    And gives the weary rest.
John Newton (1725-1807)

25. I am not skilled to understand
    What God has willed, what God has planned;
    I only know at His right hand stands
    One who is my Saviour.
Dora Greenwell (1821-82)

26. I am so glad that our Father in heaven
    Tells of His love in the Book He has given:
    Wonderful things in the Bible I see;
    This is the dearest that Jesus loves me.

    Though I forget Him and wander away,
    Still He doth love me wherever I stray:
    Back to His dear loving arms do I flee,
    When I remember that Jesus loves me.
Philip P. Bliss (1838-76)

27. I am trusting Thee, Lord Jesus,
   Trusting only Thee;
   Trusting Thee for full salvation,
   Great and free.

   I am trusting Thee to guide me;
   Thou alone shalt lead,
   Every day and hour supplying
   All my need.

Frances Ridley Havergal (1836-79)

28. I do not know what lies ahead,
   The way I cannot see;
   Yet one stands near to be my guide,
   He'll show the way to me:

   I know who holds the future,
   And He'll guide me with his hand;
   With God things don't just happen,
   Everything by Him is planned.
   So, as I face tomorrow,
   With its problems large and small,
   I'll trust the God of miracles,
   Give to Him my all.

Alfred B. Smith & Eugene Clarke © 1947
Singspiration Music

29. I hear the words of love,
   I gaze upon the blood,
   I see the mighty sacrifice,
   And I have peace with God.

The clouds may go and come,
And storms may sweep my sky
This blood-sealed friendship changes not;
The cross is ever nigh.

Horatius Bonar (1808-89)

30. I heard the voice of Jesus say:
    'Come unto me and rest;
    Lay down, thou weary one, lay down
    Thy head upon My breast!'
    I came to Jesus as I was,
    Weary, and worn, and sad;
    I found in Him a resting-place,
    And He has made me glad.

    I heard the voice of Jesus say:
    'Behold I freely give
    The living water; thirsty one,
    Stoop down and drink and live!'
    I came to Jesus, and I drank
    Of that life-giving stream;
    My thirst was quenched, my soul revived,
    And now I live in Him.

    I heard the voice of Jesus say:
    'I am this dark world's Light;
    Look unto Me, thy morn shall rise,
    And all thy day be bright!'
    I looked to Jesus, and I found
    In Him my star, my sun;

And in that light of life I'll walk
Till travelling days are done.

Horatius Bonar(1808-89)

31. I need Thee every hour, most gracious Lord;
    No tender voice like Thine can peace afford.

    I need Thee, O I need Thee, every hour I need Thee;
    O bless me now my Saviour; I come to Thee.

    I need Thee every hour; teach me Thy will,
    And Thy rich promises in me fulfil.

    Annie Sherwood Hawks (1835-1918)

32. I'll go in the strength of the Lord,
    In paths He has marked for my feet;
    I'll follow the light of His word,
    Nor shrink from the dangers I meet.

    His presence my steps shall attend,
    His fullness my wants shall supply;
    On Him, 'til my journey shall end,
    My unwavering faith will rely.

    Edward Turney © 1983 Salvationist Publishing

33. I'll praise my Maker while I've breath,
    And when my voice is lost in death,
    Praise shall employ my nobler powers:
    My days of praise shall ne'er be past,
    While life and thought and being last,
    Or immortality endures.

    Isaac Watts (1674-1748)

34. I'm special because God has loved me
For He gave the best thing that he had to save me
His own Son Jesus crucified
To take the blame for all the bad things I have done
Thank you, Jesus, thank you, Lord,
For living me so much.
I know I don't deserve anything
Help me feel your love right now,
To know deep in my heart
That I'm your special friend.
Graham Kendrick © 1986 Kingsway Music

35. In heavenly love abiding,
No change my heart shall fear;
And safe is such confiding,
For nothing changes here;
The storm may roar without me,
My heart may low be laid;
But God is round about me,
And can I be dismayed?

Wherever He may guide me,
No want shall turn me back;
My Shepherd is beside me,
And nothing can I lack;
His wisdom ever waketh,
His sight is never dim;
He knows the way He taketh,
And I will walk with Him.

Green pastures are before me,
Which yet I have not seen;
Bright skies will soon be o'er me,
Where the dark clouds have been:
My hope I cannot measure,
My path to life is free:
My Saviour has my treasure,
And He will walk with me.

Anna Laetitia Waring (1820-1910)

36. In the name of Jesus, we have the victory.
    In the name of Jesus, demons will have to flee.
    Who can tell what God can do?
    Who can tell of His love for you?
    In the name of Jesus, Jesus, we have the victory.

Anon

37. I've found a friend; O such a friend!
    He loved me ere I knew Him;
    He drew me with the cords of love,
    And thus He bound me to him;
    And round my heart still closely twine
    Those ties which nought can sever,
    For I am His, and He is mine, for ever and for ever.

    I've found a friend; O such a friend!
    So kind, and true, and tender!
    So wise a counsellor and guide, so mighty a defender!
    From Him who loves me now so well
    What power my soul shall sever?

Shall life or death? Shall earth or hell?
No! I am His for ever.
James Grindlay Small (1817-88)

38. Jesu, Lover of my soul,
    Let me to Thy bosom fly,
    While the nearer waters roll,
    While the tempest still is high;
    Hide me, O my Saviour, hide,
    Till the storm of life be past;
    Safe into the haven guide,
    O receive my soul at last.
Charles Wesley (1707-88)

39. Jesus calls us! O'er the tumult
    Of our life's wild restless sea,
    Day by day His voice is sounding,
    Saying, 'Christian, follow me.'

    Jesus calls us! By Your mercies,
    Saviour, may we hear Your call,
    Give our lives to Your obedience,
    Serve and love You best of all.
Cecil Frances Alexander (1823-95)

40. Jesus my Lord will love me for ever,
    From Him no power of evil can sever,
    He gave his life to ransom my soul,
    Now I belong to Him:

    Now I belong to Jesus,
    Jesus belongs to me,

Not for the years of time alone,
But for eternity.

Norman Clayton © 1943

41. Just a closer walk with Thee;
    Grant it, Jesus, this my plea;
    Daily walking close with Thee;
    Let it be, dear Lord, let it be.

    Through this world of toils and snares,
    If I falter, Lord, who cares?
    Who with me my burden shares?
    None but Thee, dear Lord, none but Thee.

Anon.

42. Just as I am without one plea
    But that thy blood was shed for me,
    And that Thou bidd'st me come to Thee,
    O Lamb of God, I come

    Just as I am, though tossed about
    With many a conflict, many a doubt,
    Fighting and fears within, without,
    O Lamb of God, I come.

    Just as I am, Thou wilt receive,
    Wilt welcome, pardon, cleanse, relieve;
    Because Thy promise I believe,
    O Lamb of God, I come.

Charlotte Elliott (1789-1871)

43. Lead kindly Light, amid the encircling gloom,
   Lead Thou me on;
   The night is dark, and I am far from home;
   Lead Thou me on.
   Keep Thou my feet; I do not ask to see
   The distant scene; one step enough for me.

   So long Thy power has blest me, sure it still
   Will lead me on
   O'er moor and fen, o'er crag and torrent, till
   The night is gone;
   And with the morn those angel faces smile
   Which I have loved long since, and lost awhile.
                    John Henry Newman (1801-90)

44. Like a river glorious is God's perfect peace;
   Over all victorious in its bright increase;
   Perfect, yet it floweth fuller every day;
   Perfect, yet it groweth deeper all the way.
   Stayed upon Jehovah hearts are fully blest;
   Finding as He promised, perfect peace and rest.
                    Frances Ridley Havergal (1836-79)

45. Lord Jesus, think of me
   And take away my fear;
   In my depression be assured
   That You are near.

   Lord Jesus, think of me
   By many cares oppressed;

In times of great anxiety
Give me your promised rest.

Lord Jesus, think of me
When darker grows the day;
And in my sad perplexity
Show me the heavenly way.

Lord Jesus, think of me
When night's dark shadows spread;
Restore my lost serenity,
And show me light ahead.

Lord Jesus, think of me,
That when the night is past
I may the glorious morning see
And share your joy at last.

Synesius of Cyrene (c.375-430)

46. Loved with everlasting love,
Led by grace that love to know;
Spirit, breathing from above,
Thou hast taught me it is so.
O this full and perfect peace!
O this transport all divine!
In a love which cannot cease
I am His and He is mine.

His for ever, only His;
Who the Lord and me shall part?
Ah, with what a rest of bliss
Christ can fill the loving heart!

Heaven and earth may fade and flee,
First-born light in gloom decline;
But, while God and I shall be,
I am His, and He is mine.
George Wade Robinson (1838-77)

47. May God's blessing surround you each day
As you trust Him and walk in His way.
May His presence within
Guard and keep you from sin,
Go in peace, go in joy, go in love.
Cliff Barrows © 1982

48. My faith looks up to Thee,
Thou Lamb of Calvary, Saviour divine:
Now hear me while I pray; take all my guilt away;
O let me from this day be wholly Thine.
Ray Palmer (1808-87)

49. My hope is built on nothing less
Than Jesus' blood and righteousness;
I dare not trust the sweetest frame,
But wholly lean on Jesus' name.

On Christ, the solid Rock, I stand;
All other ground is sinking sand.

When darkness seems to veil his face,
I rest on his unchanging grace;
In every high and stormy gale
My anchor holds within the veil.
Edward Mote (1797-1874)

50. My times are in Thy hand:
    My God, I wish them there;
    My life, my friends, my soul,
    I leave entirely to Thy care.

    My times are in Thy hand,
    Whatever they may be,
    Pleasing or painful, dark or bright,
    As best may seem to Thee.

    My times are in Thy hand:
    Why should I doubt or fear?
    My Father's hand will never cause
    His child a needless tear.

    My times are in Thy hand,
    Jesus, the crucified;
    Those hands my cruel sins had pierced
    Are now my guard and guide.

    My times are in Thy hand:
    I'll always trust in Thee;
    And, after death, at Thy right hand,
    I shall for ever be.

                                    William Freeman Lloyd (1791-1853)

51. O Love that wilt not let me go,
    I rest my weary soul in Thee:
    I give Thee back the life I owe,
    That in Thine ocean depths its flow
    May richer, fuller be.

                                    George Matheson (1842-1906)

52. O the joy of Your forgiveness,
Slowly sweeping over me;
Now in heartfelt adoration,
This praise I'll bring
To You, my King;
I'll worship You, my Lord.
Dave Bilbrough © 1988 Kingsway's Thankyou Music

53. Peace, perfect peace, in this dark world of sin?
The blood of Jesus whispers peace within.

Peace, perfect peace, with loved ones far away?
In Jesus' keeping we are safe, and they.

Peace, perfect peace, our future all unknown?
Jesus we know, and He is on the throne.
Edward Henry Bickersteth (1825-1906)

54. Rejoice the Lord is King!
Your Lord and King adore;
Mortals give thanks and sing,
And triumph evermore:
Lift up your heart, lift up your voice;
Rejoice, again I say, rejoice.

He sits at God's right hand,
Till all His foes submit,
And bow to His command,
And fall beneath His feet.
Lift up your heart, lift up your voice;
Rejoice, again I say, rejoice.
Charles Wesley (1707-88)

55. Rock of ages, cleft for me,
    Let me hide myself in Thee;
    Let the water and blood,
    From Thy riven side which flowed,
    Be of sin the double cure,
    Cleanse me from its guilt and power.

    Nothing in my hand I bring,
    Simply to Thy cross I cling;
    Naked, come to Thee for dress,
    Helpless, look to Thee for grace;
    Foul, I to the fountain fly;
    Wash me, Saviour, or I die.
                    Augustus Montague Toplady (1740-78)

56. Safe in the arms of Jesus,
    Safe on His gentle breast,
    There, by His love o'ershaded,
    Sweetly my soul shall rest.

    Jesus, my heart's dear refuge,
    Jesus has died for me;
    Firm on the Rock of Ages
    Ever my trust shall be.
                    Frances Jane van Alstyne (1820-1915)

57. Safe in the shadow of the Lord
    Beneath His hand and power,
    I trust in Him, I trust in Him,
    My fortress and my tower.

My hope is set on God alone
Though Satan spreads his snare,
I trust in Him, I trust in Him,
To keep me in His care.

Strong in the Everlasting Name,
And in my Father's care,
I trust in Him, I trust in Him,
Who hears and answers prayer.

Safe in the shadow of the Lord,
Possessed by love divine,
I trust in Him, I trust in Him,
And meet his love with mine.

© Timothy Dudley-Smith

58. Soon, and very soon,
We are going to see the King
Alleluia, alleluia,
We're going to see the King.

Anon.

59. Teach me, my God and King
In all things Thee to see;
And what I do in anything,
To do it as for Thee.

A servant with this clause
Makes drudgery divine;
Who sweeps a room as for Thy laws
Makes that and the action fine.

George Herbert (1593-1633)

60. Teach me Thy way, O Lord, teach me Thy way!
Thy gracious aid afford, teach me Thy way!
Help me to walk aright, more by faith, less by sight;
Lead me with heavenly light: teach me Thy way!

When doubts and fears arise, teach me Thy way!
When storms o'erspread the skies, teach me Thy way!
Shine through the cloud and rain, through sor-
 row, toil and pain;
Make Thou my pathway plain: teach me Thy way!

B. Mansell Ramsey (1849-1923)

61. The Lord's my Shepherd, I'll not want;
He makes me down to lie
In pastures green; He leadeth me
The quiet waters by.

Yea, though I walk in death's dark vale,
Yet will I fear none ill;
For Thou art with me, and Thy rod
And staff me comfort still.

Goodness and mercy all my life
Shall surely follow me,
And in God's house for evermore
My dwelling-place shall be.

The Scottish Psalter (1650)

62. There is a Redeemer,
Jesus, God's own Son,
Precious Lamb of God, Messiah,
Holy One.

Thank You, O my Father,
For giving us Your Son,
And leaving Your Spirit till
The work on earth is done.

Jesus, my Redeemer,
Name above all names,
Precious Lamb of God, Messiah,
O for sinners slain.

Melody Green © 1982 Birdwing Music

63. There's a way back to God
    From the dark paths of sin;
    There's a door that is open
    And you may go in:
    At Calvary's cross is where you begin,
    When you come as a sinner to Jesus.

E. H. Swinstead (?-1976)

64. There's a wideness in God's mercy,
    Like the wideness of the sea;
    There's a kindness in His justice,
    Which is more than liberty.

    There is no place where earth's sorrows
    Are more keenly felt than heaven:
    There is no place where earth's failings
    Have such kindly judgment given.

    There is plentiful redemption
    In the blood that has been shed;

There is joy for all the members
In the sorrows of the Head.

If our love were but more simple,
We should take Him at His word,
And our lives would be all sunshine
In the sweetness of our Lord.

Frederick William Faber (1814-63)

65. Through waves and clouds and storms
His power will clear thy way:
Wait Thou His time; the darkest night
Shall end in brightest day.

Paul Gerhardt (1607-76) tr. John Wesley (1703-91)

66. Thy way, not mine,
O Lord, however dark it be;
Lead me by Thine own hand,
Choose out the path for me.

Smooth let it be or rough,
It will be still the best;
Winding or straight,
It leads right onward to Thy rest.

I dare not choose my lot;
I would not if I might:
Choose Thou for me, my God,
So shall I walk aright.

Horatius Bonar (1808-89)

67. What a friend we have in Jesus,
All our sins and griefs to bear!
What a privilege to carry
Everything to God in prayer!
O what peace we often forfeit,
O what needless pain we bear —
All because we do not carry
Everything to God in prayer.
Joseph M. Scriven (1820-86)

68. When all Your mercies, O my God,
My thankful soul surveys,
Uplifted by the view, I'm lost
In wonder, love, and praise.
Joseph Addison (1672-1719)

69. When peace like a river attendeth my way,
When sorrows like sea-billows roll;
Whatever my lot You have taught me to say,
'It is well, it is well with my soul.'
Horatio Gates Spafford (1828-88)

70. Yesterday, today, forever,
Jesus is the same.
All may change but Jesus never;
Glory to his name.
Anon.

Copyright Details

Subject index

RUTHERFORD HOUSE

Rutherford House was founded in 1983 as a theological research and study centre. It seeks to advance scholarly understanding of the Christian faith and also to train those involved in Christian service and ministry. The House has a particular interest in training elders and church visitors.

Among materials produced for this purpose are *'The Eldership: A Training Manual'* together with three videos which come with leader's handbook:

'The Eldership'
'Pastoral Visitation'
'Bereavement Visitation'

Each video runs for approximately 60 minutes; workbooks can be ordered for use with them. They are designed for group training but can also be used by individuals.

Rutherford House, 17 Claremont Park,
Edinburgh EH6 7PJ
tel: 0131 554 1206
email info@rutherfordhouse.org.uk
www.rutherfordhouse.org.uk

Christian Focus Publications

STAYING FAITHFUL

In dependence upon God we seek to help make His infallible Word, the Bible, relevant. Our aim is to ensure that the Lord Jesus Christ is presented as the only hope to obtain forgiveness of sin, live a useful life and look forward to heaven with Him.

REACHING OUT

Christ's last command requires us to reach out to our world with His gospel. We seek to help fulfill that by publishing books that point people towards Jesus and help them develop a Christ-like maturity. We aim to equip all levels of readers for life, work, ministry and mission.

Books in our adult range are published in three imprints.

Christian Focus contains popular works including biographies, commentaries, basic doctrine and Christian living. Our children's books are also published in this imprint.

Mentor focuses on books written at a level suitable for Bible College and seminary students, pastors, and other serious readers. The imprint includes commentaries, doctrinal studies, examination of current issues and church history.

Christian Heritage contains classic writings from the past.

Christian Focus Publications, Ltd
Geanies House, Fearn,
Ross-shire, IV20 1TW, Scotland, United Kingdom
info@christianfocus.com
www.christianfocus.com